S0-BAK-493

SOTERIOLOGY

A DOGMATIC TREATISE ON THE REDEMPTION

BY

THE RT. REV. MSGR. JOSEPH POHLE, PH.D., D.D.

ADAPTED AND EDITED
BY

ARTHUR PREUSS

B. HERDER BOOK CO.,
15 & 17 SOUTH BROADWAY, ST. LOUIS, MO.,
AND
33 QUEEN SQUARE, LONDON, W. C.

Printed in U.S.A.

NIHIL OBSTAT

Sti. Ludovici, die 14. Octobris, 1943

Thomas V. Cahill

Censor Librorum

IMPRIMATUR

Sti. Ludovici, die 15. Octobris, 1943

✠ *Joannes J. Glennon, S.T.D.*

Archiepiscopus

Fourteenth Printing, 1955

Vail-Ballou Press, Inc., Binghamton and New York

TABLE OF CONTENTS

INTRODUCTION

Christology deals with the Person of our Divine Redeemer; Soteriology (περὶ τῆς σωτηρίας λόγος) considers the object for which He came into this world. This object was the Redemption of the human race.

Christ became our Redeemer or Mediator solely by His vicarious atonement, therefore, redemption (mediation) and vicarious atonement are interchangeable terms.

The fallen race of Adam was not simply restored as a whole to its original state of bliss. In order to share in the graces of the Redemption each individual human being must co-operate with the Redeemer. To be able to do this man needs (1) a teacher, who authoritatively instructs him in the truths necessary for salvation; (2) a priest who effectively applies to him the merits of the atonement; and (3) a king or shepherd, who, by the promulgation of suitable laws and precepts, guides him on the way to Heaven.

Hence our Divine Lord exercises a threefold function or office, namely (1) that of Teacher, (2) that of High Priest, and (3) that of King or Shepherd. Cfr. John XIV, 6: "I am the way (King), and the truth (Teacher), and the life (Priest)."

Soteriology, therefore, naturally falls into two main divisions: I. The Work of Redemption; II. The Three Offices of the Redeemer.

PART I
THE WORK OF REDEMPTION

PREFATORY REMARKS

The Redemption could not have been effected by a mediator who was either mere God or mere man. It required one who was both God and man. Christ, alone, being both God and man, was in a position to act as natural and moral mediator and to reconcile the human race to its Creator.

We have shown in a previous treatise that Christology [1] is founded on the doctrine of the Hypostatic Union. Similarly, Soteriology turns on the pivotal concept of the mediatorship of Christ and may be said to be implicitly contained in 2 Cor. V, 19: "God indeed was in Christ, reconciling the world to himself."

We have, therefore, to consider: (Ch. I), the mediatorship of Christ, the possibility of the Redemption, its congruity and necessity, and, by way of a corollary, the highly interesting question whether or not the Incarnation was absolutely

1 Pohle-Preuss, *Christology, A Dogmatic Treatise on the Incarnation.*

preordained; (Ch. II), the fact of the Redemption, its reality, its properties, and the concrete mode of its realization. In connection with the last-mentioned point we shall also treat (Ch. III) of Christ's Descent into hell and His Resurrection from the soteriological point of view.

CHAPTER I

CHRIST'S MEDIATORSHIP AS A CONDITION OF OUR REDEMPTION

SECTION I

THE POSSIBILITY OF THE REDEMPTION

1. DEFINITION OF THE TERM "MEDIATOR."—A mediator (*mediator,* μεσίτης) is one who holds a neutral position between parties at variance, and is therefore apt to interpose between them as the equal friend of each.

a) Thus, in the political domain, a neutral government sometimes intervenes between quarrelling powers by proffering its friendly offices as arbitrator.

The notion of a mediator, therefore, comprises two distinct elements, *viz.:* (1) The existence of two extremes in contrary opposition, and (2) a quality or characteristic proper to him who interposes, which enables him to reconcile the parties at variance.

This is the true Catholic notion of mediatorship. There is also an heretical one, which appears in the religious systems of the Gnostics and the Arians. To exalt the Creator of the universe as far as possible above mere matter, which they regarded as intrinsically evil, the Gnostics invented a series of "intermediate beings," which they called aeons, and which were supposed to bridge the gap between the Godhead and the material world. The last of these in a descending line was the so-called Demiurge, who as creator of the material universe was believed to be the proper mediator between the absolute Being and the physical cosmos.[2] The Arians regarded the Logos as the most exalted of creatures and as creator of all the rest, and ascribed to him the office of mediator between God the Father and the universe created by the Logos. We have already disproved this error by showing, in our treatises on the Divine Trinity[3] and the Incarnation,[4] that, so far from being a creature, the Logos is true God, consubstantial (ὁμοούσιος) with the Father.

b) A duly qualified mediator may exercise his functions either in the moral or in the ontological order.[5] In some manner or other moral always presupposes ontological mediation, and hence the one cannot be conceived apart from the other.

To perform the part of a moral mediator one must be able, either by one's natural powers, or through the instrumentality of grace, to reconcile opposing extremes in the order of being. Hence the distinction between

2 For a refutation of this dualistic error see Pohle-Preuss, *God the Author of Nature and the Supernatural*, pp. 17 sq.

3 Cfr. Pohle-Preuss, *The Divine Trinity*, 2nd ed., pp. 49 sqq., St. Louis 1915.

4 Cfr. Pohle-Preuss, *Christology*, pp. 10 sqq.

5 *In ordine morali sive ethico;* in *ordine ontologico sive essendi.*

mediator naturalis and *mediator per gratiam*. Moses,[6] the Levites, the Prophets, and the Apostles were mediators by grace. So is every Catholic priest in virtue of his ordination. As regards natural mediatorship, Christ is our only Mediator in the moral order, because He is the sole natural Mediator between God and man. "The fact of Christ's existence is in itself a mediation, a bond between the Creator and His creatures. By uniting our humanity to His Divinity, He united us to God and God to us. He is of God and in God, but He is also of us and in us."[7] Being consubstantial with man as well as with God,[8] Christ is the born mediator between God and man (*mediator naturalis*).

This unique natural mediatorship constitutes the foundation of an equally unique moral mediatorship. The offended Deity exacted adequate atonement for the sins of mankind, and therefore redemption or moral mediation was impossible except on the basis of a natural mediatorship.[9]

c) It follows, by way of a corollary, (1) that mankind has but one mediator, because there is no natural mediator between God and man other than the Godman Jesus Christ; (2) that all other so-called "mediators" are such merely by grace. They owe their mediatorial power solely and entirely to Christ, and can consequently be called mediators only in a subordinate and secondary sense.

6 Cfr. Deut. V, 5: "*Medius fui inter Dominum et vos*—I stood between the Lord and you."

7 Wilhelm-Scannell, *A Manual of Catholic Theology*, Vol. II, p. 140, 2nd ed., London 1901.

8 Cfr. Pohle-Preuss, *Christology*.

9 V. *infra*, Sect. 2.

No further argument is required to disprove the Protestant objection that Catholics obscure and degrade the unique mediatorship of Christ by admitting a host of priests and saints as co-mediators between God and man. "It is an essential function of the office of a mediator," says Aquinas, "to join together and unite those between whom he is to interpose; for it is in the middle that extremes meet. Now, to unite men with God perfectively belongs to Christ, through whom men are reconciled to God. . . . And therefore Christ alone is a perfect mediator between God and men, inasmuch as, by His death, He reconciled the human race to God. . . . There is, however, nothing to forbid others from being called mediators between God and men under a certain respect (*secundum quid*), in so far, namely, as they cooperate in uniting men with God, either by disposing them for such a union (*dispositive*), or by assisting them in the process of unification (*ministerialiter*)."[10]

2. THE DOGMA.—Theologically speaking, Mediation is synonymous with Redemption. That Christ was our natural Mediator is an article of faith, defined by the Council of Trent. *"Si quis hoc Adae peccatum [originale] . . . per aliud remedium asserit tolli quam per meritum unius mediatoris Domini nostri Iesu Christi, qui nos*

10 "*Ad mediatoris officium proprie pertinet coniungere et unire eos, inter quos est mediator; nam extrema uniuntur in medio. Unire autem homines Deo perfective quidem convenit Christo, per quem homines sunt reconciliati Deo. . . . Et ideo solus Christus est perfectus Dei et hominum mediator, inquantum per suam mortem humanum genus Deo reconciliavit. . . . Nihil tamen prohibet aliquos alios secundum quid dici mediatores inter Deum et homines, prout scil. cooperantur ad unionem hominum cum Deo dispositive vel ministerialiter.*" *S. Theol.*, 3a, qu. 26, art. 1.—Cfr. Franzelin, *De Verbo Incarnato*, thes. 46, Rome 1881.

Deo reconciliavit in sanguine suo . . . anathema sit." Anglice: "If any one asserts that this sin of Adam [original sin], . . . is taken away . . . by any other remedy than the merit of the one Mediator, our Lord Jesus Christ, who hath reconciled us to God in His own blood, . . . let him be anathema." [11]

a) Moral mediation, or the Redemption proper, according to Holy Scripture, consists in the shedding of the blood of Him who was the sole, because the natural, Mediator between God and man. Consequently, Christ's moral mediatorship is based upon His natural mediatorship. Cfr. Col. I, 19 sq.: "*Quia in ipso* [*scil. Christo*] *complacuit omnem plenitudinem inhabitare* [= *mediatio ontologica naturalis*] *et per eum reconciliare omnia in ipsum pacificans per sanguinem crucis eius* [= *mediatio moralis*]— Because in him it hath well pleased the Father, that all fulness should dwell; and through him to reconcile all things unto himself, making peace through the blood of his cross." [12] Both the ontological and the moral mediatorship of Christ are pregnantly summed up by St. Paul in 1 Tim. II, 5 sq.: "*Unus enim Deus, unus*

11 *Conc. Trid.*, Sess. V, can. 3 (in Denzinger's *Enchiridion Symbolorum, Definitionum et Declarationum in Rebus Fidei et Morum*, ed. Bannwart, n. 790, Friburgi 1908).

12 For a full explanation of this text cfr. J. N. Schneider, *Die Versöhnung des Weltalls durch das Blut Jesu Christi nach Kol. I, 20*, Ratisbon 1857.

et mediator Dei et hominum,[13] *homo Christus Iesus, qui dedit redemptionem semetipsum pro omnibus*[14]— For there is one God, and one mediator of God and men, the man Christ Jesus, who gave himself a redemption for all."

The Redemption of the human race began with the conception of Jesus Christ and was consummated in the shedding of His precious Blood on the Cross.[15] Hence the functions of His moral mediatorship comprise all His human-divine (theandric) acts from the manger to Calvary. His mediatorial act *par excellence* was the institution of the New Covenant. "*Et ideo Novi Testamenti mediator*[16] *est, ut morte intercedente in redemptionem earum praevaricationum, quae erant sub priori Testamento, repromissionem accipiant*—And therefore he is the mediator of the New Testament: that by means of his death, for the redemption of those transgressions which were under the former testament, they that are called may receive the promise of eternal inheritance."[17] In fact everything that Christ did and does for us must be regarded as the result of His mediatorship, *e. g.*, the institution of the Holy Sacrifice of the Mass, the establishment of His Church, the mission of the Holy Ghost, the sanctification of souls,[18] etc.

b) We meet with a profound conception of Christ's mediatorship in the writings of St. Augustine. This Father may be said to have anticipated the objections of such later heretics as

13 εἷς καὶ μεσίτης Θεοῦ καὶ ἀνθρώπων.

14 ὁ δοὺς ἑαυτὸν ἀντίλυτρον ὑπὲρ πάντων.

15 Cfr. Heb. X, 5 sqq.

16 διαθήκης κοινῆς μεσίτης.

17 Heb. IX, 15.

18 Cfr. John XIV, 6.

Calvin, who held that Christ is our mediator only according to His Divinity, and the older Lutheran theologians, who attributed His mediatorial action exclusively to His human nature.[19]

The truth lies between these extremes. It is the God-man as such who is our Mediator, but only in His human nature. "He is the mediator between God and man," says St. Augustine, "because He is God with the Father, and a man with men. A mere man could not be a mediator between God and man; nor could a mere God. Behold the mediator: Divinity without humanity cannot act as mediator; nor can humanity without Divinity; but the human Divinity and the Divine humanity of Christ is the sole mediator between Divinity and humanity."[20] And again: "Christ is the mediator [between God and man] not because He is the Word; for the Word, being immortal and happy in the highest degree, is far removed from the miseries of mortal men; but He is the mediator *as man*."[21]

c) The Schoolmen went into the matter even more deeply by resolving the concept of mediation into its constituent elements.

19 Cfr. Bellarmine, *De Christo*, V, 1–10.

20 "*Mediator Dei et hominum, quia Deus cum Patre, quia homo cum hominibus. Non mediator homo praeter deitatem, non mediator Deus praeter humanitatem. Ecce mediator: divinitas sine humanitate non est mediatrix, humanitas sine divinitate non est mediatrix, sed inter divinitatem solam et humanitatem solam mediatrix est humana divinitas et divina humanitas Christi.*" *Serm.*, 47, c. 12, n. 21.

21 "*Non ob hoc mediator est Christus, quia Verbum; maxime quippe immortale et maxime beatum Verbum longe est a mortalibus miseriis; sed mediator est secundum quod homo.*" *De Civ. Dei*, IX, 15. For additional Patristic texts see Petavius, *De Incarn.*, XII, 1–4; Vasquez, *Comment. in S. Theol.*, III, disp. 83, c. 1.

They had to meet this logical difficulty: The idea of natural mediation essentially implies three distinct elements, *viz.:* the two extremes God and man, and a mediator who must be both God and man, *i. e.,* God-man (θεάνθρωπος). Christ, being God according to His Divine Nature, is identical with the first of these two extremes. Consequently, He cannot be a true and natural mediator, for it is impossible to conceive Him as a go-between between Himself and man. Cfr. Gal. III, 20: "A mediator is not of one."

The Scholastics retorted that Christ is the mediator between God and man not *qua* Logos, but *qua* Word Incarnate, *i. e.* as man. Cfr. 1 Tim. II, 5: "One mediator of God and men, the man Christ Jesus." The God man Christ Jesus is not only numerically distinct from all other men, He is likewise hypostatically distinct from the Father and the Holy Ghost, being a different Person than either. Hence His mediatorship involves three distinct factors: God, man, and Christ. It is true that, regarded in His Divine Nature, as God, Christ is the mediator between Himself and mankind. But his mediation is not effected by the Godhead as such, it is effected solely by His manhood, which is hypostatically united with the Second Person of the Trinity. This gives rise to seeming paradoxes, *e. g.:* As man He adores, as God He is adored; as man He gives satisfaction, as God he receives it; as man He offers sacrifices, as God He accepts them. But this two-sidedness does not destroy the reality of Christ's natural and moral mediation. It simply constitutes its substratum. To postulate a numerical distinction between the Divine Nature of Christ and the Godhead of the Father and the Holy Ghost, would be to base the possibility of the atonement on Tritheism.[22]

22 Cfr. St. Thomas, *S. Theol.,* 3a, qu. 26. art. 2.

SECTION 2

CONGRUITY AND NECESSITY OF THE REDEMPTION

1. CONGRUITY OF THE REDEMPTION.—Inasmuch as an end can be best attained by congruous means, *i. e.*, means specially adapted to that particular end, the "congruous" may be said to be "morally necessary." But it is never necessary in the strict metaphysical sense of the term. Failure to employ a merely congruous means does not necessarily frustrate the end to be attained; nor does it argue a moral fault. A wise man knows how to attain his ends by various means, none of which may be positively "incongruous." It is in this light that we must regard certain profound arguments by which Fathers and theologians have tried to show the congruity of the Incarnation for the purpose of Redemption. Here are the more notable ones.

a) God in His exterior operation aims solely at the manifestation of His attributes for the purpose of His own glorification. What more effective means could He have chosen for this end than the Incarnation?

In the Incarnation the seemingly impossible was effected. The Creator was inseparably united with the creature, the Infinite with the finite, omnipotence with mercy; Heaven and earth were locked together, as it were, by the bond of the Hypostatic Union. Man is a microcosm reflecting the whole created universe. No doubt this is what Tertullian had in mind when he wrote: "The Son of God was born; I am not ashamed, because men must needs be ashamed [of it]. And the Son of God died; it is by all means to be believed, because it is absurd. And after having been buried, He rose again; the fact is certain, because it is impossible."[1]

(α) God's justice and mercy are glorified in the Incarnation, because, despite their diametric contrariety, they both meet in it, in such manner that either attribute works itself out to the full extent of its infinity without disturbing the other.[2] When, moved by infinite mercy, the Son of God satisfied infinite justice by expiating the sins of mankind on the Cross, "justice and peace kissed" in very truth.[3]

(β) God's love, too, triumphantly manifested itself in the Incarnation of the Logos. "God so loved the world, as to give his only begotten Son."[4] The mystery of the Incarnation gives the lie to Aristotle, who held that, owing to the impassable gulf separating man from God, anything like "friendship" is impossible between them. "Both he that sanctifieth, and they who are sanctified, are all of one; for which cause he is not ashamed to call them brethren."[5]

(γ) Divine wisdom also reached its climax in this sublime mystery. "If any one will diligently consider the mystery of the Incarnation," says St. Thomas, "he

1 "*Natus est Dei Filius: non pudet, quia pudendum est; est mortuus Dei Filius: prorsus credibile, quia ineptum est; et sepultus resurrexit; certum est, quia impossibile.*" *De Carne Christi*, c. 5.

2 Cfr. Pohle-Preuss, *God: His Knowability, Essence, and Attributes*, pp. 466 sqq.

3 Ps. LXXXIV, 11.

4 John III, 16.

5 Heb. II, 11.

will find [therein] a profundity of wisdom exceeding all human understanding. . . . Hence it is that he who piously meditates on this mystery, will constantly discover [therein] new and more wonderful aspects." [6]

b) Why did the Second Person of the Most Holy Trinity become incarnate, rather than the First or the Third? There is a profound reason for this.

We have pointed out in Christology [7] that nothing in the personal traits of the Father or of the Holy Ghost would forbid either of these Divine Persons to assume human flesh. But there is that in the personal character of the Son which makes it more appropriate for Him to become incarnate than either the Father or the Holy Ghost. It was through the Logos that the universe was created; [8] and what is more fitting than that it should also be repaired by His agency? [9] Moreover, as the Logos alone is "the [perfect] image of God," [10] it was highly appropriate that He should restore to its pristine purity God's likeness in men, which had been destroyed by sin.[11] "The Divine Logos Himself came into this world," says St. Athanasius, "in order that, being the image of the Father, He might restore man, who was created to His image and likeness." [12] It also befit-

6 "*Si quis autem diligenter incarnationis mysterium consideret, inveniet tantam sapientiae profunditatem, quod omnem humanam cognitionem excedat. . . . Unde fit, ut pie consideranti semper magis ac magis admirabiles rationes huiusmodi mysterii manifestentur.*" *Contr. Gent.*, IV, 54.

7 Pohle-Preuss, *Christology*, pp. 135 sq.

8 Cfr. John I, 3.

9 Pope St. Leo the Great says: "*. . . ut, quoniam ipse est, per quem omnia facta sunt et sine quo factum est nihil, . . . cuius erat conditor, etiam esset reformator.*" (*Serm.*, 64, Migne, *P. L.*, LIX, 358.)

10 Cfr. 2 Cor. IV, 4.

11 Cfr. Gen. I, 26.

12 *Or. de Incarn. Verbi*, 13.

ted the hypostatic character of the Son of God that, as the true son of the Virgin Mary, He should become the "Son of man," in order to reconstitute all men "sons of God" as by a new birth.[13] The second of these momenta is well brought out by St. Augustine when he says: "That men might be born of God, God was first born of them. For . . . He through whom we were to be created, was born of God, and He by whom we were to be re-created, was born of a woman." [14] St. John of Damascus emphasizes the first-mentioned point when he observes: "The Son of God also became the son of man; He took flesh from the Blessed Virgin, but did not cease to be the Son of God." [15]

c) It strikes us as an admirable manifestation of divine wisdom that the Son of God assumed human nature rather than that of the angels. Heb. II, 16: *"Nusquam enim angelos apprehendit, sed semen Abrahae apprehendit* [16]— For nowhere doth he take hold of the angels: but of the seed of Abraham he taketh hold."

By assuming flesh, the Son of God wished to reconstruct human nature upon its own foundations and to propose to man for his imitation a pattern exemplar in the "Following of Christ,"— neither of which objects could have been attained had the Divine Logos assumed the nature of an angel.

13 Cfr. John I, 12; Gal. IV, 4 sq.

14 "*Ut homines nascerentur ex Deo, primo ex ipsis natus est Deus. Christus enim . . . natus ex Deo, per quem efficeremur, et natus ex femina, per quem reficeremur.*" *Tract. in Ioa.*, 2, n. 15.

15 "*Filius Dei etiam filius hominis fit, qui ex s. virgine incarnatus est, nec tamen a filiali proprietate discessit.*" *De Trinitate*, 1.— Cfr. St. Thomas, *S. Theol.*, 3a, qu. 3, art. 8.

16 ἐπιλαμβάνεται.

One of the most telling reasons why it was more appropriate for the Son of God to assume the nature of man than that of the angels[17] is that none but a God-man could endow the created universe with the highest degree of perfection of which it was capable. By the hypostatic incorporation into the Godhead of a nature composed of a material body and a spiritual soul, the physical universe was linked with the realm of pure spirits. "In no other way," says Lessius, "could the whole universe have been so appropriately perfected . . . for by the assumption of man the whole universe was after a fashion assumed into and united with the Godhead."[18] Thus Christ is in very deed both the natural and the supernatural keystone of the cosmos, the beginning and the end of all things, the pivot of the universe. Cfr. 1 Cor. III, 22: "*Omnia enim vestra sunt . . . vos autem Christi, Christus autem Dei* — For all things are yours, . . . and you are Christ's, and Christ is God's."

d) It is a further proof of divine wisdom that the Son of God chose to come into this world as the child of a virgin rather than as a full-grown man.

A sweet infant is more apt to win our affection than a mature man. The virgin birth represented the realization of the last of the four possible modes in which a human being can come into existence. Three of these had already been realized in Adam, Eve, and their descendants. Adam was created immediately by God (*sine*

17 On the possibility of the Logos' assuming the nature of an angel, see Suarez, *De Incarn.*, disp. 14, sect. 2.

18 *De Perfect. Moribusque Divinis*, XII, 4.

mare et femina); Eve sprang from the male without female co-operation (*ex mare sine femina*); their descendants are propagated by sexual generation (*ex mare et femina*); Jesus Christ alone originated from a woman without male co-operation (*ex femina sine mare*). This fact guarantees the reality and integrity of our Lord's human nature, as has been shown in Christology.[19]

By His incorporation into the race of the "first Adam," our Blessed Redeemer became the "second Adam"[20] in a far higher sense than if He had appeared on earth in a celestial body. There is a similar antithesis between Eve and the Blessed Virgin Mary. In Christ the male was elevated, ennobled, and consecrated; in Mary, the female. "He did not despise the male," says St. Augustine, "for he assumed the nature of a man, nor the female, for he was born of a woman."[21]

2. Necessity of the Redemption.—Necessity is twofold: absolute or hypothetical. The latter may be subdivided into a number of special varieties. Hence in treating of the necessity of the Redemption we shall have to distinguish between several hypotheses.

a) Wyclif asserted that the Redemption was an absolute necessity. This proposition is untenable.[22]

19 Pohle-Preuss, *Christology*, pp. 41 sqq.

20 Cfr. Rom. V, 14 sqq.; 1 Cor. XV, 45.

21 "*Nec mares fastidivit, quia marem suscepit; nec feminam, quia ae femina factus est.*" *Ep.*, 3. On the propriety of Christ's becoming incarnate at the particular time when He was conceived by the Blessed Virgin Mary, cfr. Saint Thomas, *S. Theol.*, 3a, qu. 1, art. 5–6.— On the whole subject of this subdivision cfr. De Lugo, *De Myst. Incarn.*, disp. 1, sect. 2; Suarez, *De Incarn.*, disp. 3, sect. 3; Chr. Pesch, *Praelect. Dogmat.*, Vol. IV, 3rd ed., pp. 209 sqq.

22 Cfr. Denzinger-Bannwart, *Enchiridion*, n. 607.

Whatever is absolutely necessary involves the same kind of certainty as that two and two are four. To ascribe such mathematical necessity to the Incarnation would be to deny the liberty of the Redemption as well as that of the Creation, for the creation of the world was an indispensable condition of the Incarnation. Furthermore, Revelation clearly teaches that the Redemption of the human race was in the strictest and most perfect sense of the word a work of divine grace, mercy, and love. Wyclif is wrong in holding that the Incarnation satisfies a legitimate demand of human nature, for in that hypothesis reason would be able to demonstrate with mathematical certainty the possibility and existence of the Hypostatic Union, which we know is not the case. So far is the human mind from being able to understand this mystery, that it cannot even demonstrate it after it has been revealed.[23] Hence the Incarnation, if it was at all necessary, could be necessary only in an hypothetic sense, that is, on some condition or other. What may this condition be?

b) Raymond Lull, Malebranche, Leibniz, and other champions of absolute Optimism contend that when God determined to create the universe, He of necessity also decreed the Incarnation, because it is inconceivable that He should have wished to deprive His work of its highest perfection. In other words, the concept of "the best possible world" includes the Incarnation.

This theory, which destroys the liberty of the Creator, is refuted in our dogmatic treatise on *God the Author*

23 Cfr. Pohle-Preuss, *Christology*, pp. 45 sq.

of Nature.[24] Here we merely wish to point out two facts: that the Creator Himself, without regard to the future Incarnation, described His work as "very good,"[25] and that the Incarnation would not be preeminently a free grace if it corresponded to a strict claim of nature.

The champions of moderate or relative Optimism[26] maintain that the present order, capped by the Incarnation, represents the "best possible world," not because the Incarnation was a metaphysical necessity, but because it was morally necessary in view of God's superabundant goodness. These writers forget that, while the Incarnation represents the apogee of divine glorification and the highest perfection of the universe, it involves at the same time an equally great humiliation and self-abasement (*exinanitio*, κένωσις) of God's Majesty, which is inconceivable in any other hypothesis except as a free decree of His love.[27]

c) The further question arises: Did God owe it to fallen man to redeem him by means of the Incarnation? The answer is that the restoration of the state of grace which man had enjoyed in Paradise was just as truly a free gift of God's mercy and benevolence as that state itself, nay, even more so.

That God was under no obligation to redeem His creatures is evidenced by the fate of the fallen angels. Cfr. also Wisd. XII, 12: "*Quis tibi imputabit, si peri-*

24 Cfr. Pohle-Preuss, *God the Author of Nature and the Supernatural*, pp. 45 sq.

25 Gen. I, 31.

26 *E. g.*, Didacus Ruiz (*De Volunt. Dei*, disp. 9), Sylvester Maurus (*De Deo*, disp. 51), and Viva (*De Incarn.*, qu. 2, art. 2).

27 Cfr. De Lugo, *De Myst. Incarn.*, disp. 2, sect. 1–2.

erint nationes, quas tu fecisti? — Who shall accuse thee, if the nations perish, which thou hast made?" St. Augustine may have held harsh and exaggerated views on the subject of predestination, but he was certainly right when he said: "The entire mass incurred penalty; and if the deserved punishment of condemnation were rendered to all, it would without doubt be righteously rendered." [28]

To say that the Incarnation, though the result of a free decree, was the only means God had of redeeming the human race,[29] would be unduly to restrict the divine attributes of mercy, wisdom, and omnipotence in their essence and scope.[30] God might, without injustice, have left the human race to perish in its iniquity, and there is nothing repugnant either to faith or right reason in the assumption that He might, with or without the intervention of some appointed saint or angel as representative of the

28 "*Universa massa poenas dabat, et si omnibus damnationis supplicium redderetur, non iniuste procul dubio redderetur.*" (*De Nat. et Grat.*, c. 5.)

29 This opinion was held by St. Anselm (*Cur Deus Homo?* I, 4; II, 12), Richard of St. Victor (*De Incarn. Verbi*, c. 8), and Tournely (*De Deo*, qu. 19, art. 1; *De Incarn.*, qu. 4 sqq.). It is absolutely without Scriptural warrant. De Lugo says of it: "*Mihi videtur satis ad errorem accedere, eo quod, licet non omnino clare, fere tamen clare ex Scriptura colligatur oppositum, accedente praesertim expositione communi Patrum.*" (*Op. cit.*, disp. 2, sect. 1, n. 6). Lately an attempt has been made to interpret St. Anselm's opinion more mildly (Dörholt, *Die Lehre von der Genugtuung Christi*, pp. 201 sqq., Paderborn 1891). For a criticism of Dörholt's position see Stentrup in the *Zeitschrift für katholische Theologie*, pp. 653 sqq., Innsbruck 1892. B. Funke, *Grundlagen und Voraussetzungen der Satisfaktionstheorie des hl. Anselm*, Münster 1903, furnishes a notable contribution in support of Dörholt's thesis. Cfr. also L. Heinrichs, *Genugtuungstheorie des hl. Anselmus*, Paderborn 1909; and Pohle-Preuss, *God: His Knowability, Essence, and Attributes*, pp. 462 sqq.

30 "*Sunt stulti qui dicunt: Non poterat aliter sapientia Dei homines liberare, nisi susciperet hominem et nasceretur de femina. . . . Quibus dicimus: Poterat omnino, sed si aliter faceret, similiter vestrae stultitiae displiceret.*" (St. Augustine, *De Agone Christi*, XI, 12). For other Patristic texts consult Petavius, *De Incarn.*, II, 13.

whole race, have restored penitent sinners to His grace without demanding any equivalent whatever, or on the basis of an inadequate satisfaction. Hence, according to Suarez,[31] the universal teaching of theologians that God in His omnipotence might have repaired human nature in a variety of other ways,[32] is so certain that "it cannot be denied without temerity and danger to the faith."

d) The Incarnation can be conceived as a necessary postulate of the Redemption only on the assumption that God exacted adequate (*i. e.*, infinite) satisfaction for the sins of men. In that hypothesis manifestly none but a natural mediator, that is to say, a Godman, was able to give the satisfaction demanded.

Sin involves a sort of infinite guilt and cannot be adequately atoned for except by an infinite satisfaction.[33] The Fathers held that not even the human nature of Christ, as such, considered apart from the Hypostatic Union, could make adequate satisfaction for our sins; much less, of course, was any other creature, human or angelic, equal to the task. For, in the words of St. Augustine, "we could not be redeemed, even by the one Mediator between God and men, the man Christ Jesus, if He were not also God." [34]

Though this was the most difficult mode of redemption,

31 *De Incarn.*, disp. 4, sect. 2, n. 3.

32 Cfr. St. Thomas, *S. Theol.*, 3a, qu. 1, art. 2: "*Deus per suam omnipotentem virtutem poterat humanam naturam multis aliis modis reparare.*"

33 Cfr. St. Thomas, *S. Theol.*, 3a, qu. 2, ad 2.

34 St. Augustine, *Enchir.*, c. 108: "*Neque per ipsum liberaremur unum mediatorem Dei et hominum, hominem Iesum Christum, nisi esset et Deus.*"— For additional texts from the writings of the Fathers consult Vasquez, disp. 4, c. 3; Thomassin, *De Incarn.*, I, 4.

it was the one actually chosen by God. The Incarnation of the Logos satisfied the full rigor of His justice, but it also gave free play to His boundless love. The fact that the atonement was decreed from eternity explains such Scriptural phrases as John III, 14: "*Exaltari oportet*[35] *Filium hominis* — The Son of man must be lifted up" (as Moses lifted up the serpent in the desert), and Luke XXIV, 26: "*Nonne haec oportuit pati*[36] *Christum* — Was it not necessary for Christ to have suffered these things?"[37]

35 ὑψωθῆναι δεῖ.

36 ἔδει παθεῖν.

37 Cfr. Heb. IX, 22.— On the subject of the foregoing paragraphs consult J. Kleutgen, *Theologie der Vorzeit,* Vol. III, pp. 336 sqq., 381 sqq., 430 sqq., Münster 1870; Chr. Pesch, *Praelectiones Dogmaticae,* Vol. IV, 3rd ed., pp. 201 sqq., Friburgi 1909; De Lugo, *De Myst. Incarn.,* disp. 2, 3, 5; Billuart, *De Incarn.,* diss. 3, art. 2; B. Dörholt, *Die Lehre von der Genugtuung Christi,* pp. 171 sqq., Paderborn 1891.

SECTION 3

PREDESTINATION OF THE REDEEMER

1. STATE OF THE QUESTION.—Would the Son of God have appeared in the flesh if Adam had not sinned? In other words, was the Incarnation absolutely predetermined? This is a most interesting question, and the famous theological controversy to which it gave rise, throws so clear a light on the dogma of the Redemption and the sublime dignity of the Redeemer, that we must give an account of it here.

The underlying problem may be briefly stated as follows: The Incarnation was dictated by two principal motives, namely, (1) compassion for the misery of mankind, and (2) the glorification of God and His Christ.[1] Which of these motives outweighed the other? This question must receive an answer before we can determine whether the fall of Adam was an indispensable condition of the Incarnation, or whether the Divine Logos assumed human flesh irrespective of the existence or non-existence of a sinful race of

1 Cfr. John XVII, 4 sqq.; 2 Thess. I, 12.

men. The former view is held by the Thomists, the latter by the Scotists.

The Scotists conceive the divine decrees appertaining to the Redemption in the following order. First of all comes the absolute predistination of Christ and His divine kingdom, consisting of angels and men. In the second place, the permission of the sin of Adam; and in the third place, the mission of Christ in His capacity of passible Redeemer.

The Thomists, on the other hand, hold that God created the universe without regard to Christ; that He subsequently decreed to permit sin, and lastly determined on the Incarnation of the Logos for the purpose of redeeming the human race.

As may be seen from this enumeration, the Scotists put the Incarnation first, while the Thomists put it last. From the Scotist point of view God's predominant motive in decreeing the Incarnation was the dignity and glorification of Christ. The universe was created for Christ's sake. The Thomists, on the other hand, ascribe the Incarnation of the Logos primarily to God's mercy. In the Scotist hypothesis the Incarnation is altogether independent of the Fall; the Thomists regard the latter as an indispensable condition of the former.

Against the Scotist view there lies this objection: If Christ was not predestined to atone for the sins of men, why did He appear on earth as a passible Redeemer rather than, as we should have every reason to expect, in the capacity of an impassible, glorified Godman? The Scotists meet this difficulty by saying that the first and absolute decree touching the Incarnation was modified in view of the Fall; that after the Fall, Christ, who originally was to have appeared among men as *homo gloriosus,* decided to assume human flesh and become *homo passibilis.*

In general terms the two theories may be characterized as follows: The Scotistic theory is inspired by a transcendent idealism, whereas the Thomist view conforms to the facts as we know them. To enable the reader to form his own estimate we will briefly state the leading arguments adduced by both schools.

2. THE THOMISTIC THEORY.—That the Fall of Adam was the chief motive which prompted God to decree the Incarnation, is held by all Thomists,[2] and also by a large number of theologians belonging to other schools, *e. g.,* Gregory of Valentia, Vasquez, Petavius, Cardinals Toletus and De Lugo, and even by the "ideal" Lessius.[3] Among modern theologians this theory has been espoused by Kleutgen,[4] Stentrup,[5] Tepe,[6] and many others.

Toletus and Petavius absolutely reject the Scotist hypothesis. Chr. Pesch[7] and L. Janssens[8] prefer the Thomist view, but admit the other as probable. In this they follow St. Thomas himself[9] and St. Bonaventure.[10] The Angelic Doctor both in his Commentary on the *Liber Sententiarum* and in the *Summa Theologica* expresses

2 Cfr. Billuart, *De Incarn.,* diss. 3, art. 3.

3 *De Praedest. Christi* (Opusc., t. II, pp. 483 sqq., Paris 1878).

4 *Theologie der Vorzeit,* Vol. III, pp. 393 sqq.

5 *Soteriologia,* thes. 2.

6 *Instit. Theol.,* Vol. III, pp. 663 sqq., Paris 1896.

7 *Praelect. Dogm.,* Vol. IV, 3d ed., pp. 216 sqq.

8 *De Deo-Homine, II: Soteriologia,* pp. 44 sqq.

9 *Comment. in Quatuor Libros Sent.,* III, dist. 1, qu. 1, art. 3.

10 *Comment. in Quatuor Libros Sent.,* III, dist. 1, art. 2, qu. 2.

himself with cautious reserve. St. Bonaventure says: "He who was made flesh for us alone knows which of the two theories is the better. Which is to be preferred it is difficult to say, because both are Catholic and sustained by Catholic authors." [11]

The Thomistic conception is based upon arguments which, though not cogent, are perfectly sound.

a) St. Thomas himself argues as follows: "Some claim that the Son of God would have assumed human flesh even if man had not sinned. Others assert the contrary, and their teaching seems to have a greater claim to our assent. The reason is this. Whatever proceeds solely from the Divine Will, transcending every exigency of nature, must remain unknown to us, except it be revealed by Sacred Scripture. . . . Now, Sacred Scripture invariably assigns the sin of Adam as the motive of the Incarnation. It is more befitting, therefore, to regard the Incarnation as ordained by God for the cure of sin, so that if there had been no sin there would have been no Incarnation." [12]

As a matter of fact, whenever Sacred Scripture speaks of the motive of the Incarnation, it invariably points to

[11] *l. c.* Cfr. R. Guardini, *Die Lehre des hl. Bonaventura von der Erlösung*, Düsseldorf 1921.

[12] *S. Theol.*, 3a, qu. 1, art. 3: "*Quidam dicunt, quod etiamsi homo non peccasset, Dei Filius incarnatus fuisset. Alii vero contrarium asserunt, quorum assertioni magis assentiendum videtur. Ea enim quae a sola Dei voluntate proveniunt supra omne debitum naturae, nobis innotescere non possunt, nisi quatenus in S. Scriptura traduntur. . . . Unde quum in S. Scriptura ubique incarnationis ratio ex peccato primi hominis assignetur, convenientius dicitur, incarnationem opus ordinatum esse a Deo in remedium contra peccatum, ita quod peccato non existente incarnatio non fuisset.*"

the sin of Adam. It is because He was sent to redeem the fallen race of men that Christ received the name of "Jesus," *i. e.*, Saviour or Redeemer (*salvator, σωτήρ*). Cfr. Matth. I, 21: "*Et vocabis nomen eius Iesum; ipse enim*[13] *salvum faciet populum suum a peccatis eorum* — And thou shalt call his name Jesus; for he shall save his people from their sins."[14] Jesus Himself never even hints at any other motive. Cfr. Luke XIX, 10: "*Venit enim Filius hominis quaerere et salvum facere, quod perierat* — For the Son of man is come to seek and to save that which was lost." It seems perfectly legitimate to conclude, therefore, that the redemption of man was the main motive which prompted God to send His Son. Had there been a higher and more comprehensive motive, it would be strange to find no hint of it in the Scriptures.

The weight of this argument must not, however, be overrated. For, in the first place, the texts upon which it is based are purely affirmative, but not exclusive, so that the argument based upon them is at bottom merely one *ex silentio*. And, secondly, the Scriptural passages in question all refer to the actual order of salvation, not to its hidden background. Although the Incarnation and the Redemption are causally correlated, Sacred Scripture does not define the nature of their mutual relationship, and tells us nothing at all concerning the question whether the Incarnation is subordinate to the Redemption, or *vice versa*.

b) Owing to their larger knowledge of the writings of the Fathers, modern theologians are

13 *γάρ*.

14 Similarly Matth. IX, 13; Mark II, 17; Luke I, 31; John III, 17; Rom. III, 25; Gal. IV, 4; 1 Tim. I, 15; 1 John III, 5.

able to construct a far more convincing Patristic argument than was possible in the time of St. Thomas. Holy Scripture merely intimates by its silence that there would have been no Incarnation if Adam had not sinned. The Fathers enunciate this proposition in explicit terms.

"I am persuaded," writes Cardinal Toletus, "that, had the old Scholastic doctors been acquainted with the many Patristic testimonials which I now adduce, they would have admitted that the contrary view is absolutely devoid of probability."[15] We will cite a few of these testimonials. St. Athanasius says: "The assumption of human nature [on the part of the Logos] presupposes a necessity, apart from which He would not have put on flesh."[16] St. Ambrose asks: "What was the cause of the Incarnation if not this, that the flesh which had sinned by itself, should by itself be redeemed?"[17] And St. Augustine declares that "the Lord Jesus Christ came in the flesh . . . for no other reason than . . . to save, liberate, redeem, and enlighten [those who are engrafted members of His body]."[18] We may also refer to the Creed: "Who for us men and for our salvation descended from Heaven," and to the Easter hymn: "O happy fault, which deserved to have so great and glorious a Redeemer!"

To sum up the argument: Tradition, so far as we

[15] *In S. Theol., h. l.*

[16] *Or. contr. Arian.*, 2, 54. Similarly Gregory of Nazianzus (*Or.*, 30, n. 3) and Cyril of Alexandria (*Thesaur.*, V, 8).

[17] "*Quae erat causa incarnationis, nisi ut caro, quae per se peccaverat, per se redimeretur?*" *De Incarn.*, c. 6, n. 56.

[18] *De Pecc. Mer. et Rem.*, I, 26, 39.— Additional Patristic texts in Lessius, *De Praedest. Christi*, sect. 1, n. 5; Stentrup, *Soteriologia*, thes. 1 sq. Cfr. Petavius, *De Incarn.*, II, 17.

are able to ascertain it, is against the absolute predestination of Christ, but holds that, if man had not sinned, the Son of God would never have become incarnate.

To escape this argument, the Scotists urge their above-mentioned distinction between "*Christus gloriosus*" and "*Christus passibilis.*" God's original decree concerning the Incarnation, they say, was from all eternity modified by the Fall of man, which necessitated a passible redeemer; and it is to this particular aspect of the Incarnation alone that the Patristic texts apply; at least it is possible so to interpret them. But even if they could be interpreted in the wider sense in which they are understood by the Thomists, we should still be dealing with a mere *theory,* which no rule of faith constrains us to adopt. In support of this view the Scotist theologians point to the modification which the Patristic theory of "satisfaction" has experienced in course of time without detriment to its substance.

3. The Scotistic Theory.—If the question at issue had to be decided purely on the authority of theologians, we should be unable to arrive at a unanimous decision, so evenly is authority balanced against authority. The Scotistic theory originated with Abbot Rupert of Deutz.[19] It was adopted by Albert the Great[20] and developed by Duns Scotus,[21] in whose school it eventually obtained the upper hand.[22] It has also found many ardent defenders outside the Scotistic

19 *De Gloria et Hon. Filii Hominis Libri XIII; De Trinit.*, III, 20.

20 *Comment. in Quatuor Libros Sent.*, III, dist. 20, art. 4.

21 *Comment. in Quatuor Libros Sent.*, III, dist. 7, qu. 3.

22 Cfr. Mastrius, *Disp. Theol.*, disp. 4, qu. 1.

camp, among them Ambrose Catharinus,[23] Ysambert, St. Bernard of Siena, St. Francis de Sales,[24] and especially Suarez.[25] For a while its defenders were few, but of late the theory is again coming into favor. Among its modern champions we may mention: Faber, Gay, Bougaud, Schell, Fr. Risi, and Du Cappucce.[26]

The arguments for the Scotist position are undeniably strong.

a) Their Scriptural basis is the oft-repeated statement of St. Paul that the Incarnation of Christ was pre-ordained by an eternal and absolute divine decree without regard to the Fall.

The Apostle declares that all things are *by* Christ and *for* Christ, *i. e.,* tend towards Him as their final end and object. Cfr. Heb. II, 10: "*Propter quem omnia et per quem omnia* — For whom are all things and by whom are all things."[27] Col. I, 16 sqq.: "*Omnia per ipsum et in ipso*[28] *creata sunt . . . et ipse est ante omnes*[29] *et omnia in ipso constant; et ipse est caput corporis Ecclesiae, qui est principium,*[30] *primogenitus ex mortuis, ut sit in omnibus ipse primatum tenens*[31] — In him were all things created . . . and he is before all, and by him all things consist. And he is the head of the body, the church, who is the beginning, the first-born from the dead; that in all things he may hold the

23 *De Praedestin. Eximia Christi,* Lugduni 1542.

24 *De l'Amour de Dieu,* II, 4.

25 *De Incarn.,* disp. 5.

26 *Études Franciscaines,* 1890, 1900; cfr. Chr. Pesch, S. J., *Das Sühneleiden unseres göttl. Erlösers,* pp. 113 sqq.

27 δι' ὅν τὰ πάντα καὶ δι' οὗ τὰ πάντα.

28 εἰς αὐτόν.

29 πρὸ πάντων.

30 ἀρχή.

31 πρωτεύων.

primacy." If Christ holds first place in the divine economy of the universe, and the world of angels and men was reserved to the last, so runs the Scotist argument, the Incarnation cannot have been subordinate to the Creation and Redemption, but, on the contrary, must rank far above it. Without Christ there could have been no creation. Hence Christ is "before all," "the first-born of every creature."[32] He is the centre and pivot of the universe, not in consequence of the Fall, but absolutely and from all eternity. He has not been added to the created universe by accident, but rules it as *πρωτεύων*, and is the Alpha and Omega of all things from the beginning.[33]

b) Though this theory cannot be strictly demonstrated from the writings of the Fathers, yet the Patristic interpretation of several passages in the Sapiential Books of the Old Testament seems to lend it weight. The fact that the Fathers were unable to gauge the full bearing of their interpretation does not forbid us to push to their legitimate conclusions the principles which they asserted.

We have pointed out in our treatise on the Trinity[34] that certain of the Fathers applied Proverbs VIII, 22: "The Lord possessed me in the beginning of his ways, before he made anything from the beginning,"[35] to the temporal birth of the Logos, that is, the Incarnation. This can only mean that Christ was predestined to be

32 Col. I, 15; cfr. Rom. VIII, 29.

33 The objections urged against this interpretation may be read in De Lugo, *De Myst. Incarn.*, disp. 7, sect. 2.

34 Pohle-Preuss, *The Divine Trinity*, p. 157.

35 "*Dominus possedit* (ἔκτισε) *me in initio viarum suarum, antequam quidquam faceret a principio.*"

the First and that all things were created for His sake.[36]

On the strength of Gen. II, 24 and Eph. V, 31 sqq. several Fathers held that the nature of matrimony, as an image of "Christ's union with His Church," was revealed to Adam in Paradise. If this be true, our Lord's appearance on earth cannot be conceived as conditioned by the Fall. "Even if man had not sinned, but had remained in the state of innocence," says St. Augustine,[37] "matrimony would still be the symbol of Christ's union with His Church."[38]

When it comes to theological arguments, the Scotists can allege in their favor all the reasons which we have given above for the congruity of the Incarnation as such, especially the fact that, in the words of Lessius,[39] "by the assumption of man the whole universe was, after a fashion, assumed into and united with the Godhead." Strangely enough, Lessius subsequently undermined his own position by saying: "If any created nature was to be assumed primarily for the sake of perfecting the universe, it would have been the most perfect, *i. e.*, that of the highest angel."[40] This conclusion does not follow. Unlike man, an angel is not a "microcosm." Besides, there is something sublime and over-

36 Cfr. Suarez, *De Incarn.*, disp. 5, sect. 2.

37 "*Coniugium etiam in statu innocentiae, si homo non peccasset, futurum sacramentum coniunctionis Christi cum Ecclesia.*" (*De Nupt. et Concup.*, I, 21.)

38 For the Thomist reply to this argument see Lessius, *De Praedest. Christi*, n. 23 sqq.

39 *De Perfect. Mor. Div.*, XII, 4.

40 *De Praedest. Christi*, n. 9.

whelming in the thought that, as Scotism consistently teaches, not only all men but all angels, not only fallen and sinful man, but likewise man as constituted in Paradise, owe their original sanctity entirely to the merits of an absolutely predestined Redeemer; that all grace radiates from Christ, the "sun of justice," who sanctifies angels and men and disperses the shadows of death.

Perhaps the weightiest argument adduced for the Scotist position is the one developed by Suarez: The end cannot be inferior to the means devised for its attainment. This would be the case if the Incarnation merely served the purpose of the Redemption. Christ is not only the crown of the created universe, He is also the climax of divine glorification. Without Him the universe would be meaningless. He who is highest and most perfect in the order of being, must also be first in the plan of creation, and the fulness of divine glory cannot have been dependent on the accident of the Fall.

The Scotistic theory recommends itself by its sublimity. It groups angels and men around the Godman as the center of the universe, the highest and final revelation, the beginning and end of all things.[41]

41 Hugon, *Revue Thomiste*, May-June, 1913; P. Chrysostom, O. F. M., *Le Motif de l'Incarnation et les Principaux Thomistes Contemporains*, Tours (Marcel Cattier), 1921 (an able statement of the Scotist position).—L. J. Walker, S.J., *Why God Became Man*, New York 1921.—J. P. Arendzen, *Whom Do You Say—?* London 1927.

CHAPTER II

THE REDEMPTION OF THE HUMAN RACE THROUGH CHRIST'S VICARIOUS ATONEMENT

SECTION I

THE REALITY OF CHRIST'S VICARIOUS ATONEMENT

ARTICLE I

VICARIOUS ATONEMENT DEFINED

This Chapter deals with the concrete fact of Christ's vicarious atonement (*satisfactio vicaria*) rather than with the abstract notion of Redemption, which even heretics do not entirely deny; hence we must be careful to define our terms.

1. EXPLANATION OF THE TERM "ATONEMENT."—a) By atonement we understand the reparation of any wrong or injury, either material (*damnum*) or moral (*offensa, iniuria*). Material injury demands restitution; moral injury can be repaired only by satisfaction or atonement in the strict sense of the term. The Roman Catechism defines "satisfaction" as "nothing else than compensation for an injury offered to another." Satisfaction in the sense of discharging

a penance enjoined in confession will be treated in connection with the Sacrament of Penance.

b) Atonement, in the sense in which the term is used in Soteriology, presupposes an offence committed against, or an injury done to, God. It is for our sins that God demands satisfaction. Sin and satisfaction are consequently correlative terms, or, to put it more accurately, they are antitheses clamoring for reconciliation.

The concept of sin contains a twofold element: guilt (*reatus culpae*) and punishability (*reatus poenae*). Guilt and punishability are inseparable. Their gravity depends partly on the dignity of the person offended (*gravitas formalis*) and partly on the character of the offence committed (*gravitas materialis*). God is infinite in dignity and majesty; therefore every grievous sin, morally considered, involves an infinite offence. "A sin committed against God," says St. Thomas, "partakes in a manner of infinity, through its relation to the infinite majesty of God; for an offence is the more serious, the greater the person offended." [1]

Considered as a moral delinquency on the part of man, sin is a merely finite evil. In respect of God, however, it is infinite. *"Iniuria est in iniuriato."* This applies, of course, only to mortal sin, which seriously disturbs the sinner's relation to

[1] *S. Theol.,* 3a, qu. 1, art. 2, ad 2.

God. This relation, if justice be given free scope, cannot be restored except by means of adequate satisfaction (*emptio, redemptio*).

c) Grievous sin, as we have said, involves an infinite offence, for which no creature, least of all the sinner himself, can render adequate satisfaction. Adequate in this case means infinite satisfaction, and infinite satisfaction can be given only by one who is infinite in dignity. Hence none but a Godman could redeem the human race. Hence also the necessity of a vicarious atonement.

2. Definition of "Vicarious Atonement."—The notion of *vicariatio* does not imply that he who acts as substitute or representative for another takes upon himself the other's guilt or sin as such. No one can be the bearer or subject of another's sins. In this erroneous sense vicarious atonement involves a contradiction, because no mediator can give satisfaction for another's sins unless he is himself sinless. Vicarious atonement, therefore, can only mean the voluntary assumption of a punishment due to sin,—not indeed the *reatus poenæ,* which implies real guilt, but the penance imposed by God. In other words, the Godman renders infinite satisfaction in our stead, and this satisfaction by its objective worth counterbalances our infinite offence and is ac-

cepted by God as though it were given by ourselves.

To illustrate the case by an analogy. The human race is like an insolvent merchant. Christ voluntarily assumes our obligations and is compelled to pay the whole debt. The sum of this debt is His Precious Blood. (1 Pet. I, 18 sq.)

3. Objections Refuted.—The Socinians, and modern Rationalists generally, reject the Catholic dogma of Christ's vicarious atonement on the pretext that it involves manifest contradictions, (a) with regard to God, (b) with regard to Christ, and (c) with regard to man. We will briefly examine these alleged contradictions.

a) The doctrine of the atonement is held to be contradictory in respect of God for the reason that forgiveness of sins is sometimes attributed to pure mercy and sometimes to strict justice, whereas these two attributes are mutually exclusive.

If the simultaneous manifestation of God's infinite mercy and justice really involved an intrinsic contradiction, St. Paul would have been the first to incur this charge, for he says in his Epistle to the Romans: "You are justified freely by his grace,[2] through the redemption [3] that is in Christ Jesus." [4] In exacting satisfaction for our sins from His own Son instead of us poor sinners, God exercised in an eminent manner both His mercy and His justice. There is no contradiction involved in this proposition. This would be the case only if the sinner were held to give adequate satisfaction in

[2] δωρεὰν τῇ αὐτοῦ χάριτι. [3] διὰ τῆς ἀπολυτρώσεως. [4] Rom. III, 24.

person and his performance subsequently stamped as a grace. Holy Scripture is perfectly consistent in teaching, on the one hand, that "God so loved the world as to give his only-begotten Son,"[5] and, on the other, that "by sending his own Son, in the likeness of sinful flesh, and of sin, [God] hath condemned sin in the flesh."[6]

b) The doctrine of the atonement is declared to be contradictory for the further reason that it involves the punishment of an innocent person in lieu of the guilty criminal. It is downright murder, however disguised, for God to exact the blood of His own guiltless Son in expiation for the sins of others, say the Rationalists.

God would indeed be unjust had He imposed the guilt and punishment of others upon His innocent Son as though He were the guilty criminal. But this is by no means the teaching of the Church. Not having personally sinned, Christ could not be punished as a sinner. Hence His death was not a punishment in the proper sense of the word, but merely a *satisfactio laboriosa*. Furthermore, it was not imposed on Him against His will. He Himself declares: "I lay down my life for my sheep. . . . I lay it down of myself,[7] and I have power to lay it down: and I have power to take it up again."[8] *Volenti non fit iniuria* (No wrong arises to one who consents). Hence the atonement cannot be said to involve a violation of commutative justice. Nor does it run counter to distributive justice, for Christ's dolorous passion and death, besides redounding to the advantage of the human race, also brought Him personal reward and glory. Cfr. Luke XXIV, 26: "Ought not

5 John III, 16.

6 Rom. VIII, 3.— Cfr. Pohle-Preuss, *God: His Knowability, Essence, and Attributes*, pp. 466 sqq.— Another objection, based on the immutability of God, is discussed in the appendix to this volume, *infra*, pp. 165 sq.

7 ἀπ' ἐμαυτοῦ.

8 John X, 15, 18.

Christ to have suffered these things, and so to enter into his glory?"

c) In regard to man, the doctrine of the atonement is denounced as repugnant on the score that one who is guilty of a crime should, as a point of honor, give the necessary satisfaction himself, and not shift this painful duty to another. Our Rationalist adversaries add that the idea of a man's appropriating to himself the fruits of another's labor is preposterous. They overlook the fact that man was absolutely unable to render adequate satisfaction for sin. God manifested His infinite love and mercy precisely in deigning to accept a *vicarious* atonement. It cannot be proved that this involves an injustice. The objection will lose much of its force if we take into consideration the fact that Christ represented the human race in the order of grace in much the same manner in which Adam had vicariously represented it upon the occasion of the Fall. Hence the Scriptural antithesis between the "first Adam" and the "second Adam." Christ is no stranger to us; He is "bone of our bone," our "brother" as well as our spiritual head. His merits constitute as it were a family heirloom, in which each of us has a share.

The privilege of participating in the merits of Christ's vicarious atonement does not relieve us of the duty of personally atoning for our sins. That Christ has rendered adequate satisfaction for the sins of the whole race, does not mean that each individual human being is *eo ipso* subjectively redeemed. This is the teaching of "orthodox" Lutheranism, not of the Catholic Church. We Catholics believe that the individual sinner must feel sorry for his sins, confess them, and render satisfaction for them,— though, of course, no satisfaction can be of any avail except it is based on the merits of our Lord and Saviour Jesus Christ.[9]

ARTICLE 2

THE DOGMA OF CHRIST'S VICARIOUS ATONEMENT PROVED FROM REVELATION.

1. VARIOUS HERESIES AND THE TEACHING OF THE CHURCH.—The heretical opinions that have arisen in course of time with regard to the dogma of Christ's vicarious atonement owe their inspiration either to Rationalism or to Pantheism. The Rationalist error that the idea of individual liberty absolutely excludes original sin, found its embodiment in Pelagianism and Socinianism, two heretical systems which, though not contemporaneous, agreed in denying original sin and the atonement. Pantheism, which merges all individuals into one Absolute Being and regards sin as a function of the Godhead, gave birth to Gnosticism and modern Theosophy.

a) All these heresies are based on a radically wrong conception of the nature of sin.

α) Pelagianism rests on the fundamental fallacy

9 Cfr. *Conc. Trident.*, Sess. XIV, cap. 8 (Denzinger-Bannwart, *Enchiridion*, n. 904). An excellent treatise on the philosophical aspects of the atonement is G. A. Pell's *Das Dogma von der Sünde und Erlösung im Lichte der Vernunft*, Ratisbon 1886. Edw. von Hartmann's specious objections (see that writer's book, *Die Krisis des Christentums in der modernen Theologie*, pp. 10 sqq., Berlin 1882) are effectively refuted by B. Dörholt, *Die Lehre von der Genugtuung Christi*, pp. 160 sqq.. Paderborn 1891.

that sin is essentially the free act of an individual and cannot be conceived as moral guilt incurred by propagation (original sin). In consequence of this basic error, the Pelagians wrongly held that the grace of Christ has for its object not the redemption of the whole human race by the effacement of an inherited sin of nature, but the setting up of an ideal or pattern of virtue in accordance with which the individual is obliged to regulate his personal conduct. Christ gave us "a good example" to counteract the "bad example" set by Adam. Pelagianism credited the sinner with sufficient strength to arise after falling, nay to attain to a state of perfect sinlessness[1] without supernatural aid, and hence denied the necessity of grace and unduly exaggerated the moral capacity of human nature.[2]

The soteriological consequences implied in Pelagius' system were expressly drawn by Socinianism. This heresy originated towards the close of the sixteenth century by way of a reaction against "orthodox" Protestantism. Its founders were Laelius Socinus and his nephew Faustus, both natives of Siena, Italy. Faustus Socinus (1539–1604) systematized and developed the teachings of his uncle in several works: *De Christo Servatore, De Officio Christi,* and *Brevis Discursus de Ratione Salutis*

1 *Impeccantia, ἀναμαρτησία.*

2 Cfr. Blunt's *Dictionary of Sects, Heresies, Ecclesiastical Parties, and Schools of Religious Thought,* pp. 415 sqq., New Impression, London 1903; also the Preface to P. Holmes' translation of *The Anti-Pelagian Works of Saint Augustine,* Vol. I, pp. i sqq., Edinburgh 1872. St. Augustine treats at length of Pelagianism in the following books: *De Nuptiis et Concupiscentia, Contra Duas Epistolas Pelagianorum, Enchiridion, De Gratia et Libero Arbitrio, De Correptione et Gratia, De Praedestinatione Sanctorum, De Dono Perseverantiae, Contra Iulianum Pelagianum, De Gestis Pelagii, De Octo Dulcitii Quaestionibus, Comment. in Psalmos, Serm.,* x and xiv, and in his Epistles to Paulinus, Optatus, Sextus, Celestine, Vitalis, and Valentine. Cfr. also the *Varia Scripta et Monumenta ad Pelagianorum Historiam Pertinentia* at the close of Vol. X of the Benedictine edition of St. Augustine's works.

Nostrae ex Sermonibus Fausti Socini.[3] Socinianism denied the Trinity, the Divinity of Jesus Christ, the necessity of supernatural grace, and the dogma of the vicarious atonement. Its champions alleged that Christ is properly speaking neither our Saviour nor a true high priest, but merely a teacher pointing the way to salvation. The chief object of His coming was to inculcate the "Our Father." To the Socinians have succeeded the modern Unitarians, who are distinguished from their predecessors principally by the denial of the miraculous conception of our Lord and the repudiation of His worship. The Socinian theology also had considerable influence in forming the modern Rationalist school.[4]

Hermes and Günther[5] held an intermediate position between the Catholic dogma and these heretical vagaries.

β) Diametrically opposed to the soteriological teaching of the Pelagians and Socinians is that of the Gnostics and Theosophists.

Gnosticism was at bottom a Manichæan heresy. Its votaries held that, since the human soul is part of that principle (*hyle*) which is essentially bad, sin cannot be a moral delinquency, and for a man to be redeemed from sin implies no more than that his soul is freed from the shackles of the material body. The human nature of Christ was regarded by the Gnostics as purely fictitious and apparitional, because the Divine Logos could not possibly unite Himself with matter, which is essentially evil.

3 These writings are collected in the *Bibliotheca Fratrum Polonorum*, Vols. 1 and 2, Irenopoli 1656.

4 Blunt, *Dictionary of Sects*, etc., p. 568. For a detailed analysis of the Socinian teaching see A. Harnack, *Dogmengeschichte*, Vol. III, 4th ed., pp. 784 sqq., Freiburg 1910.

5 On the teaching of Hermes (+ 1831) and Günther (+ 1863), cfr. J. Kleutgen, S. J., *Theologie der Vorzeit*, Vol. III, pp. 457 sqq., Münster 1870.

In such a system, needless to say, there was no room for the Redemption, much less for a vicarious atonement.

Theosophy is subject to similar delusions. Being radically Pantheistic, it regards sin as a cosmic factor of equal necessity and importance with virtue. Good and evil to the Theosophist are two world-powers endowed with equal rights. Sin is merely a limitation of infinity. The Absolute Being alone, conceived as an impersonal spirit, is unbounded and sinless. Each individual human soul is part and parcel of the Absolute, and as such its own God. In other words, the Deity becomes incarnate in every human being. The human race may be said to have been redeemed by Christ only in the sense that He was the first to enlighten men on the true relationship between the finite and the infinite, between good and evil. The real redemption of man consists in his re-absorption into the infinite ocean of being, out of which he has temporarily emerged like a foam-crested wave.[6]

b) Though the Church has never formally (*in terminis*) defined the doctrine of the vicarious atonement,[7] she has nevertheless inculcated the substance of it so often and so vigorously that it may be said to be one of the cardinal dogmas of the Catholic religion. The Third General Council of Ephesus (A. D. 431) solemnly defined: "If any one therefore says that [Christ] offered Him-

6 On modern Theosophy cfr. Madame Blavatky's *Isis Unveiled*, *The Secret Doctrine*, and *Key to Theosophy;* also the numerous writings of Annie Besant, especially her *Esoteric Christianity;* A. P. Warrington, art. "Theosophy" in the *Encyclopedia Americana*, Vol. XV; E. R. Hull, S. J., *Studies in Theosophy*, 2nd ed., Bombay 1905; J T. Driscoll in the *Catholic Encyclopedia*, Vol. XIV, pp. 628 sqq.

7 Cfr. K. Martin, *Conc. Vatican. Document. Collectio*, p. 37, Paderborn 1873.

self up as a sacrifice for Himself, and not solely for us,[8] let him be anathema." [9] Still more clearly the Council of Trent: "If any one asserts that this sin of Adam . . . is taken away . . . by any other remedy than the merit of the one Mediator, our Lord Jesus Christ, who hath reconciled us to God in His own blood, made unto us justice, sanctification and redemption, . . . let him be anathema." [10] In another place the same Council says: "[Christ] by His most holy passion on the wood of the Cross merited justification for us and made satisfaction for us unto God the Father." [11] The last-quoted phrase closely resembles the technical terminology of the Schools.

2. Proof from Sacred Scripture.—The vicarious atonement is clearly inculcated both by the Old and the New Testament, though not, of course, in the technical terms of modern theology.

a) Isaias gives graphic expression to it in the

[8] καὶ οὐχὶ δὴ ὑπὲρ μόνων ἡμῶν. Here is the whole passage in Latin: "*Si quis ergo dicit, quod pro se obtulisset* [*Christus*] *semetipsum oblationem et non potius pro nobis solis, anathema sit.*"

[9] *Conc. Ephes.*, can. 10 (Denzinger-Bannwart, *Enchiridion*, n. 122). — Cfr. the *Decretum pro Iacobitis* (*ibid.*, n. 711).

[10] "*Si quis hoc Adae peccatum . . . per aliud remedium asserit tolli quam per meritum unius mediatoris D. N. Iesu Christi, qui nos Deo reconciliavit in sanguine suo, factus nobis iustitia, sanctificatio et redemptio, . . . anathema sit.*" *Conc. Trident.*, Sess. V, can. 3 (Denzinger-Bannwart, n. 790).

[11] "*Qui . . . sua sanctissima passione in ligno crucis nobis iustificationem meruit et pro nobis Deo Patri satisfecit.*" *Conc. Trident.*, Sess. VI, cap. 7 (Denzinger-Bannwart, n. 799). We use Waterworth's translation.

famous prophecy which describes the suffering of the "Servant of God."

The Messianic character of this prophecy is sufficiently established by such New Testament texts as Mark XV, 28, Luke XXII, 37, Acts VIII, 33, 1 Pet. II, 22 sqq.[12] We quote its salient passages: "Surely he hath borne our infirmities, and carried our sorrows, and we have thought him as it were a leper, and as one struck by God and afflicted. But he was wounded for our iniquities, he was bruised for our sins; the chastisement of our peace was upon him, and by his bruises we are healed. All we like sheep have gone astray, every one hath turned aside into his own way; and the Lord hath laid on him the iniquity of us all. He was offered [13] because it was his own will,[14] and he opened not his mouth; he shall be led as a sheep to the slaughter. . . . For the wickedness of my people have I struck him. . . . Because his soul hath labored, he shall see and be filled; by his knowledge shall this my just servant justify many, and he shall bear their iniquities . . . he hath borne the sins of many, and hath prayed for the transgressors." [15] The vicarious character of the "Servant's" suffering is asserted no less than eight times in this passage: (1) "He hath borne our infirmities;" (2) He has "carried our sorrows;" (3) "He was wounded for our iniquities;" (4) "He was bruised for our sins;" (5) The "chastisement of our peace was

12 The argument is well developed by A. J. Maas, S. J., *Christ in Type and Prophecy*, Vol. II, pp. 231 sqq., New York 1895.

13 The Masoretic text has, *he was called upon*. (Cfr. Maas, *l. c.*, p. 240, note.)

14 On certain textual difficulties connected with the Hebrew word na'aneh, see Maas., *l. c.*, p. 241, note.

15 Is. LIII, 4–12.

upon him;"[16] (6) "By his bruises we are healed;" (7) "The Lord hath laid on him the iniquity of us all;" (8) "He was offered because it was his own will."[17] The passage furthermore embraces all the essential elements of Christ's vicarious atonement, to wit: (a) the substitution of the innocent Messias for guilty sinners; (b) the resulting remission of punishment and healing of the evil-doers; (c) the manner in which He made satisfaction, *i. e.*, His sacrificial death.[18]

b) The New Testament inculcates the dogma of the vicarious atonement both directly and indirectly.

a) The texts which teach it directly nearly all employ the phraseology of, and are dependent upon, Isaias. Take, *e. g.*, the exclamation of John the Baptist recorded in John I, 29: "Behold the Lamb of God, behold him who taketh away the sin of the world." The passage reads as follows in the original Greek: "Ἴδε ὁ ἀμνὸς τοῦ Θεοῦ ὁ αἴρων τὴν ἁμαρτίαν τοῦ κόσμου." The ἁμαρτία τοῦ κόσμου is original sin. The verb αἴρειν, like the Hebrew words נָשָׂא and סָבַל employed by Isaias,[19] besides *tollere, i. e.*, to take away, also means *ferre* or *portare, i. e.*, to assume or bear for another.

St. Peter no doubt had the prophecy of Isaias

16 That is: The punishment which was to procure our peace with God and with men, was inflicted on him.

17 In this clause the prophet rather describes the detail of the Servant's sufferings than insists on its vicarious character; but this, too, may be inferred from the nature of the suffering. Cfr. Maas, *Christ in Type and Prophecy*, Vol. II, p. 240, note.

18 Cfr. F. Feldmann, *Der Knecht Gottes in Isaias*, Ch. 40-55, Freiburg, 1907.

19 Is. LIII, 4 and 11.

in mind when he wrote: "Who his own self bore our sins[20] in his body upon the tree . . . by whose stripes you were healed. For you were as sheep going astray; but you are now converted to the shepherd and bishop of your souls."[21] This text clearly inculcates Christ's vicarious atonement and describes its concrete realization (His death on the Cross).

St. Paul is equally clear. Cfr. 2 Cor. V, 21: "Him, who knew no sin, he hath made sin for us, that we might be made the justice of God in him." The graphic phrase ὑπὲρ ἡμῶν ἁμαρτίαν ἐποίησεν αὐτόν either means: He hath made him who was sinless a sinner, or, more probably, He hath made him who was sinless a sacrifice for sin.[22] In either case St. Paul asserts the dogma of Christ's vicarious atonement.[23]

Special importance attaches to the many New Testament texts which speak of man as being "bought" or "purchased" by the Precious Blood of Christ. Cfr. 1 Cor. VI, 20: "For you are bought with a great price." 1 Pet. I, 18 sq.: ". . . you were not redeemed[24] with corruptible things as gold and silver, . . . but with the precious blood of Christ, as of a lamb unspotted and undefiled." These terms are borrowed from

20 ἀνήνεγκεν.

21 1 Pet. II, 24 sq.

22 ἁμαρτία = *sacrificium pro peccato.* Cfr. Gal. III, 13.

23 Cfr. R. G. Bandas, *The Master-Idea of St. Paul's Epistles on the Redemption*, Bruges 1925.

24 ἐλυτρώθητε. Cfr. Rom. III, 24, Eph. I, 7, 1 Tim. II, 6.

legal and mercantile usage; they mean that men who groaned in the bondage of sin were regarded as free or redeemed by God as soon as Christ had offered His Precious Blood for them. All of which proves (1) the reality of the atonement and (2) its vicarious character.

β) Indirectly the Bible teaches the vicarious atonement in all those passages in which Christ is called the "second Adam" and contrasted with the progenitor of the human race. Cfr. Rom. V, 14 sqq.: "Death reigned from Adam unto Moses, even over them also who have not sinned after the similitude of the transgression of Adam, who is a figure of him who was to come. But not as the offence, so also the gift. For if by the offence of one, many died; much more the grace of God, and the gift, by the grace of one man, Jesus Christ, hath abounded unto many. . . . For if by one man's offence death reigned through one; much more they who receive abundance of grace, and of the gift, and of justice, shall reign in life through one, Jesus Christ. Therefore, as by the offence of one, unto all men to condemnation; so also by the justice of one, unto all men to justification of life," etc. 1 Cor. XV, 22 sqq.: "As in Adam all die, so also in Christ all shall be made alive," etc.

Adam, the physical and juridical head of the human race, sinned vicariously, because he was the representative of all; in a similar manner Jesus Christ represented the whole race when He restored it to justice. St. Paul's parallel would be meaningless if our Saviour had not acted as the representative of the entire human race when he died on the Cross. If His rôle as Redeemer had been confined to preaching and giving a good example, as the Socinians allege, what need was there of His suffering a cruel death? And if He died, not in our stead, but merely "for our benefit," why do not the Socinians acclaim the holy martyrs as so many redeemers? Christ became our "mediator" and "redeemer" in the Scriptural sense of these terms only by complementing His teaching and example by an act of true and adequate satisfaction for our sins. It is only in this sense that St. Peter, "filled with the Holy Ghost," was able to exclaim: "Neither is there salvation in any other name,"[25] and St. Paul wrote to the Corinthians: "Is Christ divided? Was Paul then [who was also a teacher of nations and a martyr] crucified for you? or were you baptized in the name of Paul?"[26] It is only in this way that the name "Jesus" receives its full significance as "Redeemer" or "Saviour" of the human race.

In view of the texts quoted it is incomprehensible how the Modernists can allege that "the doctrine of the sacrificial death of Christ is not evangelical, but originated with St. Paul." (See the Syllabus of Pius X, prop. 38).

3. Proof from Tradition.—The Fathers nearly all couched their teaching on the vicarious atonement in Scriptural terms.

a) They did not treat purely soteriological

25 Acts IV, 12.

26 1 Cor. I, 13.

questions *ex professo,* but merely adverted to them upon occasion. That the Socinians made no attempt to base their teaching upon Patristic texts, was due to the fact that Hugo Grotius had triumphantly demonstrated the vicarious atonement from the writings of the Fathers.[27] We will quote but two of the many available texts. "In accordance with the will of God," says St. Clement of Rome, "our Lord Jesus Christ gave His blood for us, and His flesh for our flesh, and His soul for our souls." [28] And St. Polycarp: "Let us ever cling to our hope and the pledge [29] of our righteousness, which is Christ Jesus, who bore our sins in His own body on the tree, . . . and endured everything for our sakes, that we might live in Him." [30]

b) On its philosophical side the dogma of the vicarious atonement underwent a process of development, as is evidenced by the part which some of the older Fathers and ecclesiastical writers assigned to the Devil.

"The question arose as follows: God and Satan are as it were two masters who contend for the possession of mankind. Hence men by departing from God fell

27 H. Grotius, *Defensio Fidei Catholicae de Veritate Satisfactionis,* published in 1614.

28 *Ep. ad Cor.,* I, 49, 6.

29 τῷ ἀῤῥαβῶνι.

30 *Ep. ad Phil.,* 8.— Many additional proofs from the writings of the Fathers are to be found in Petavius, *De Incarn.,* XII, 9 and Thomassin, *Dogm. Theol.,* IX, 7. Cfr. also Dörholt, *Die Lehre von der Genugtuung Christi,* pp. 62 sqq., Paderborn 1891 and J. F. S. Muth, *Die Heilstat Christi als stellvertretende Genugtuung,* pp. 169 sqq., Ratisbon 1904.

under Satan's power, by whom they are now kept in bondage. As, moreover, men had fallen into his power, not unwillingly, but of their own choice, may we not say that the Devil has over them a real right, a right of property and a right of conquest? Hence, when God decided to free Satan's captives, was He not bound in justice to recognize and take into consideration the Devil's rights? Many of the Fathers answered this question affirmatively."[31] St. Irenæus was the first to insist on the Devil's alleged rights.[32] Origen did not hesitate to say that Christ "ransomed us with His own blood from the power of Satan."[33] This, in itself blasphemous conception, which logically leads to the conclusion that Christ gave His blood, nay His very soul to the Devil, was rejected by Adamantius (about 300), who indignantly branded it as "all nonsense and blasphemy."[34] Saint Gregory of Nyssa followed in Origen's footsteps. But by pushing the theory to its logical conclusions, he unconsciously demonstrated its absurdity.[35] Origen's notion was formally rejected by Gregory of Nazianzus, who declared that Christ's death on the Cross effectively destroyed the tyranny of Satan. He says: "For man to be sanctified by the humanity of God, it was necessary that He Himself should free us from the tyrant, who had to be overcome by violence, and bring us back to Himself through the mediation of His

31 J. Rivière, *Le Dogme de la Rédemption*, Paris, 1905, (English translation by L. Cappadelta, in 2 vols., London 1909). The above passage is quoted from Vol. II, pp. 111 sq. of the English translation. Over one-half of the second volume is devoted to a discussion of "The Devil's Rights."

32 Cfr. Rivière-Cappadelta, *The Doctrine of the Atonement*, Vol. II. pp. 113 sqq.

33 *In Matth.*, 18, 8; *In Ioan.*, 6, 35.

34 πολλὴ βλάσφημος ἄνοια. *De Recta in Deum Fide*, I, 27 (Migne, *P. G.*, XI, 1756 sq.).

35 Cfr. Rivière-Cappadelta, *The Doctrine of the Atonement*, Vol. II, pp. 124 sqq.

Son."[36] There was a modicum of truth in Origen's theory. By the sin of our first parents Satan had become, not indeed the absolute master of the human race, but the instrument of divine wrath.[37] But when Jesus Christ, who was the Mediator between God and the human race, gave adequate satisfaction to the offended Deity, the reign of the Devil ceased. Very properly, therefore, does St. Augustine[38] attribute our release from the captivity of Satan to the sacrificial character of Christ's death on the Cross and His triumph over Satan to righteousness rather than might. "It pleased God," he says, "that in order to the rescuing of man from the power of the Devil, the Devil should be conquered, not by might, but by righteousness. . . . What, then, is the righteousness by which the Devil was conquered? What, except the righteousness of Christ? In this redemption the blood of Christ was given, as it were, as a price for us, by accepting which the Devil was not enriched, but bound, that we might be loosed from his bonds."[39] Hence, the redemption of man from the clutches of Satan did not "enrich" our arch-enemy but enslaved him, since the demands of righteousness were fulfilled. It was St. Bernard of Clairvaux who first developed this thought into the formal notion of vicarious atonement. "The prince of this world came and found nothing in the Saviour," he writes; "and when he nevertheless laid hands upon the innocent one, he rightly lost those who were his captives, when He who owed nothing to death, accepting the injury of death, rightly released him who was guilty of sin, both from the debt of death and

36 *De Agno Paschali*, 22.

37 Cfr. John XII, 31; XIV, 30; 2 Cor. IV, 4; Heb. II, 14.

38 *De Trinit.*, IV, 13.— On the teaching of St. Augustine cfr. Rivière-Cappadelta, *op. cit.*, II, 146 sqq.

39 *De Trinit.*, XIII, 13, 14, 15.

the power of the Devil. By what justice could this have been exacted from man, since it was man who owed and man who paid the debt? For 'if one died for all,' [says the Apostle, 2 Cor. V, 14], 'then all were dead': that, namely, the satisfaction of one be imputed to all . . . because the one head and body is Christ. The head therefore gave satisfaction for the members, Christ for His bowels."[40] Abélard, and especially St. Anselm, at length delivered theology from "a decaying doctrine which was now superfluous, if not actually dangerous."[41] The abuse-of-power theory made way for St. Anselm's forensic theory of satisfaction, which, after having been purged of its harsher features by St. Thomas, became the common teaching of the Schoolmen.

Theology has a right, nay the duty, to subject this theory, both in its original Patristic form and in the shape which it assumed under the hands of the medieval Scholastics, to respectful criticism. We do not deny that the theory may be defensible within certain carefully defined limits. But as onesidedly developed by the Scholastics, it does not embody the whole truth which we are able to gather from Divine Revelation. Revelation contains certain seed-thoughts which the Fathers and Schoolmen failed to appreciate at their full value. The sacrifice of the Divine Logos was dictated by infinite love and mercy as well as by strict justice. Cfr. John III, 16: "God

40 "*Venit princeps huius mundi et in Salvatore non invenit quidquam. Et quum nihilominus innocenti manus iniecit, iustissime quos tenebat amisit, quando is qui morti nihil debebat, acceptâ mortis iniuriâ iure illum, qui obnoxius erat, et mortis debito et diaboli solvit dominio. Qua enim iustitiâ id secundo ab homine exigeretur? Homo siquidem qui debuit, homo qui solvit. Nam si unus (inquit) pro omnibus mortuus est, ergo omnes mortui sunt (2 Cor. V, 14): ut videlicet satisfactio unius omnibus imputetur . . . quia caput et corpus unus est Christus. Satisfecit ergo caput pro membris, Christus pro visceribus suis.*" *De Erroribus Abaelardi*, cap. 6.

41 Rivière-Cappadelta, *op. cit.*, II, 220.

so loved the world as to give his only begotten Son."[42] God must not be conceived as an angry tyrant, who unmercifully slays his Son in order to avenge himself on the human race and thereby, as it were, to gratify the Devil, who gloats over the misfortune of others. God is just, but He is also a loving Father, who punishes His wayward children in the person of His beloved Son to show them the malice of sin by a terrible example. In other words, we cannot harmonize all the revealed elements of the atonement unless we give due emphasis to the ethical factor. The purely forensic theory of satisfaction must be supplemented and deepened by the "ethical theory of reconciliation," which accentuates God's love for Christ and the human race, and also the moral purpose of the Redemption, *i. e.,* the internal redemption of man by regeneration in God. Thus only shall we be able to refute the objections — more or less well founded — which Harnack[43] and Pfleiderer[44] have raised against the theory of satisfaction championed by the Scholastics, notably St. Anselm.

4. The Distinction Between "Satisfaction" and "Merit."—Entitatively considered, an act of satisfaction may also be a meritorious act. Nevertheless there is both a logical and a real distinction between satisfaction and merit as such. Satisfaction, in the narrower sense of the term, is reparation made for an offence, while merit may be defined as a good work performed

42 Cfr. also Eph. I, 3 sqq., II, 4 sqq.; Tit. III, 4 sq., and 1 Pet. I, 3.

43 *Grundriss der Dogmengeschichte,* 4th ed., pp. 304 sqq.

44 *Religionsphilosophie,* Vol. II, 2nd ed., Berlin 1884, pp. 467 sqq.

for the benefit of another and entitled to a reward.[45] Satisfaction supposes a creditor who insists on receiving his just dues, merit a debtor bound to give a reward. If the reward is a matter of justice, we have a *meritum de condigno,* if it is merely a matter of equity, a *meritum de congruo.*

The merits of Christ may be regarded from a fourfold point of view: (1) As to their reality, (2) as to the time when they were acquired, (3) as to their object or purpose, and (4) as to the scope of their application.

a) It is an article of faith that the Redeemer gained merits for us.

Christ, says the Tridentine Council, "merited justification for us by His most holy Passion on the wood of the Cross." The same sacred Council employs the phrase: "*Per meritum unius mediatoris Domini nostri Iesu Christi,*" and anathematizes those who say, "*Homines sine Christi iustitia, per quam nobis meruit iustificari, aut per eam ipsam formaliter iustos esse.*"[46] Isaias regarded the Redemption as a meritorious work. Is. LIII, 10: "And the Lord was pleased to bruise him in infirmity: if he shall lay down his life for sin, he shall see a long-lived seed [*i. e.,* spiritual progeny] and the will of the Lord shall be prosperous in his hand." Here satisfaction and merit are so nearly alike as to be

45 "*Meritum est opus bonum in favorem alterius mercede vel praemio dignum.*"

46 *Conc. Trid.,* Sess. VI, cap. 7; Sess. V, can. 3; Sess. VI, can. 10. Cfr. Denzinger-Bannwart, *Enchiridion,* n. 799, 790, 820.

materially identical; the Redeemer laid God under obligation while satisfying His just claims. But since He merited not only grace for us, but likewise extrinsic glory for Himself, His merits exceed the limits of the satisfaction which He gave to His Heavenly Father, because He did not need to give any satisfaction for Himself.

b) When did Christ perform His meritorious actions? In attempting to answer this question we must distinguish between the *terminus a quo* and the *terminus ad quem*.

Our Lord performed no meritorious actions (in the technical sense of the term) outside of the period of His earthly pilgrimage (*status viae*). Hence the *terminus ad quem* was the moment of His death.[47] That this is the teaching of Holy Scripture may be gathered from such texts as John IX, 4 sq.; Heb. IX, 12, X, 11 sqq. True, St. Paul teaches that the glorified Redeemer continues to "make intercession for us in Heaven."[48] But the intercession He makes for us in Heaven is based on the merits which He gained on earth and aims solely at the application of these merits to individual men.

Which was the *terminus a quo* of our Lord's meritorious actions? A man cannot perform any meritorious deeds before he has attained to the full use of reason and free-will, which generally occurs about the seventh year. In the Godman Jesus Christ, human consciousness awoke when the Godhead became hypostatically united with manhood, that is to say, at the instant of His concep-

47 The question whether this limitation of Christ's meritorious action is based upon a positive and free decree of God, or whether it is due to an intestine necessity, is purely speculative, and will be discussed in Eschatology.

48 Rom. VIII, 34; Heb. VII, 25.

tion.[49] Hence the *terminus a quo* of His meritorious actions was the first moment of His existence as God-man.[50]

c) The principal object of Christ's meritorious actions was the justification of sinners.

It is an article of faith that our Divine Saviour merited for us the forgiveness of all sins, including original sin, and, in addition, sanctifying grace. That the actual graces required for and during the process of justification also flow from the thesaurus of Christ's merits, is a theologically certain conclusion.[51] Capreolus denied it;[52] but the Tridentine Council, in teaching, "*Ipsius iustificationis exordium in adultis a Dei per Christum Iesum praeveniente gratia sumendum esse,*" evidently employs the phrase "*per Christum Iesum*" in the sense of "*per meritum Christi Iesu.*" It is likewise an article of faith that man, in the state of grace which follows justification, receives all the graces and merits which come to him solely from the treasury of the merits of Jesus Christ.[53] Our Lord Himself inculcates this by the parable of the vine and its branches.[54]

Christ also merited a reward for Himself, which consists chiefly in His extrinsic glorification after death. Cfr. Luke XXIV, 26: "*Nonne haec oportuit pati Christum et ita intrare in gloriam suam?* — Ought not Christ to have suffered these things, and so to enter into his glory?" Phil. II, 9: "*Propter quod et Deus exaltavit illum et donavit illi nomen, quod est super omne nomen* —

49 Cfr. Pohle-Preuss, *Christology,* pp. 259 sqq.

50 Cfr. Heb. X, 5.

51 Cfr. 2 Tim. I, 9.

52 Cfr. F. Stentrup, *Soteriologia,* thes. 36.

53 Cfr. *Conc. Trident.,* Sess. VI, cap. 16; Sess. XIV, cap. 8. (Denzinger-Bannwart, n. 809, 904.)

54 John XV, 5. On the grace of predestination cfr. St. Thomas, *S. Theol.,* 3a, qu. 19, art. 3.

For which cause God also exalted him, and hath given him a name which is above all names." Heb. II, 9: "*Videmus Iesum propter passionem mortis gloriâ et honore coronatum* — We see Jesus . . . for the suffering of death, crowned with glory and honor." It is consequently unscriptural to hold, as Calvin did, that Christ's love for the human race prompted Him to waive all claims to His own honor.[55]

In determining the scope of Christ's merits, Saint Thomas proceeds as follows: "Since every perfection and noble quality must be attributed to Christ, it follows that He possessed by merit whatever others possess by merit, unless it be something which would detract from His dignity and perfection more than could be gained by merit."[56] Hence, he continues, "Christ merited neither grace, nor knowledge, nor beatitude of soul, nor Divinity (*i. e.*, the Hypostatic Union). As only that can be merited which one does not yet possess, Christ would have lacked all these perfections, and therefore it is plain that He merited only such things as the glory of the body, and whatever pertains to its extrinsic excellence, *e. g.*, the ascension, adoration, etc."[57]

d) The question: Who participates in the merits of Christ? coincides with that regarding the universality of the atonement, which we shall treat below, Sect. 2, Art. 2.[58]

55 Cfr. Bellarmine, *De Christo*, V, 8–10.

56 *S. Theol.*, 3a, qu. 19, art. 3.

57 *l. c.*— Cfr. Simar, *Lehrbuch der Dogmatik*, Vol. I, 4th ed., pp. 532 sqq., Freiburg 1899.

58 On the whole subject dealt with in this subdivision of our treatise consult Pesch, *Praelectiones Dogmaticae*, Vol. IV, 3rd ed., pp. 252 sqq., Friburgi 1909.

SECTION 2

THE PROPERTIES OF CHRIST'S VICARIOUS ATONEMENT

ARTICLE 1

INTRINSIC PERFECTION OF THE ATONEMENT

Christ's vicarious atonement is intrinsically perfect and comprises within its scope all sins and all sinners.

The intrinsic perfection of Christ's vicarious atonement manifests itself in three ascending stages, which are technically called adequacy, rigorousness, and superabundance.

By adequate atonement we understand a satisfaction which completely and fully repairs the offence committed, or, at least, is accepted as a full reparation by the person offended. If the satisfaction rendered is of such high intrinsic merit that the offended person is in justice compelled to accept it, it is called rigorous. If it exceeds the offence committed, it is superabundant.

Thesis I: The satisfaction which Christ made for our sins was adequate, i. e., fully sufficient.

This thesis embodies the common teaching of a majority of Catholic theologians.

Proof. The reality of Christ's vicarious atonement is an article of faith, with which we have already dealt (*supra,* Sect. 1). In the present thesis we are merely concerned with its intrinsic properties. As the Church has never defined these, the Scotists were free to estimate them differently than the majority of Catholic divines.

The Scotists and the Nominalists hold that Christ's vicarious atonement derives its adequacy not from its own intrinsic merit, but from the accidental circumstance of its "extrinsic acceptation" by God. Suarez rejects this theory as "neither probable, nor pious, nor sufficiently in accordance with the faith."[1] This is a perfectly just criticism, since both Holy Scripture and Tradition declare that the satisfaction which Christ made for us was equivalent to the offence inherent in sin.

a) Holy Scripture distinctly declares that we were "bought" with a "price,"[2] and that this price was the Precious Blood of our Lord. Cfr. 1 Pet. I, 18 sq.: ". . . you were not redeemed with corruptible things, . . . but with the precious blood of Christ, as of a lamb unspotted and undefiled." How could the blood of Christ be called "precious" if its value was not equivalent to the offence for the reparation of which it was shed? St. Paul says: "You are bought with a great price."[3] This phrase likewise indicates that the satisfaction given by our Divine Redeemer was equivalent to the guilt of sin.

1 *De Incarn.*, disp. 4, sect. 3, n. 11.

2 *Pretium.* λύτρον.

3 *Pretio magno,* τιμῆς. 1 Cor. VI, 20.

Moreover, the Bible tells us that the Godman immolated *Himself* in expiation for our sins. Hence the satisfaction He gave to His Heavenly Father must be of equal value with Himself, and therefore, to say the least, adequate. Cfr. 1 Tim. II, 5 sq.: "There is one God, and one mediator of God and men, the man Christ Jesus: who gave himself a redemption for all (ἀντίλυτρον)." The graphic term ἀντίλυτρον, which St. Paul here employs instead of plain λύτρον, shows that he conceives "the redemption for all" as a full equivalent for sin. *"Quanta iniuria, tanta satisfactio."* In fact, it is only in this hypothesis that we can understand why the Apostle attaches such tremendous importance to the singleness of our Lord's sacrifice on the Cross, in contradistinction to the multiplicity of the ineffective offerings of the Levites. Cfr. Heb. IX, 12 and 28: "By his own blood he entered once [4] into the holies, having obtained eternal redemption. . . . So also Christ was offered once [5] to exhaust the sins of many."

b) Patristic texts in support of our thesis will be found *infra*, p. 71. A convincing theological argument for the adequacy of the atonement may be deduced from the concept of our Lord's natural mediatorship (*supra*, Ch. I, Sect. 1).

4 *Semel*, ἅπαξ.

5 *Semel*, ἅπαξ.

α) By virtue of the Hypostatic Union all human actions of the Godman are infinitely valuable in the eyes of God, independently of their extrinsic acceptation, because a theandric merit derives its full value solely from the infinite dignity of the Logos.[6] But an atonement, the expiatory power of which is, morally considered, infinite, cannot be conceived otherwise than as adequate.

β) The Scotists and the Nominalists are consequently in error when they teach that the meritorious and expiatory value of Christ's vicarious atonement, though extrinsically infinite because of its benevolent acceptation on the part of God,[7] is not so intrinsically, *i. e.*, on account of its own immanent worth.[8] Scotus' own teaching on this point is uncertain.[9] But the great majority of Scotist theologians, including such later authors as Frassen, De Rada, and Henno, undoubtedly underestimated the meritoriousness of Christ's theandric operation by asserting that it became infinitely valuable only through the condescension of God in deigning to accept it as such. The Scotists admit that Christ's human actions, because performed by the exalted person of the Godman, were invested with a certain equitable claim to

6 Cfr. Pohle-Preuss, *Christology*, pp. 161 sqq.

7 *Infinitas extrinseca ob benignam Dei acceptationem.*

8 *Infinitas intrinseca ob valorem innatum.*

9 Scotus, *Comment. in Quatuor Libros Sent.*, III, dist. 19. Hauzeur and a few other Scotists attempted to reconcile their master's teaching with the *sententia communis*, but in vain.

be received as of infinite value by a loving God; but they deny that these actions can by their own power attain to infinitude. This they declare to be impossible because these actions are essentially the product of a finite (human) nature. As the intrinsic or bullion value of a coin need not equal the extrinsic valuation stamped upon its face, they say, so the human actions of our Saviour were in themselves of a merely finite value, but capable of being raised to a higher valuation by God.

Mastrius and a few others restrict the Scotistic theory to the thesis (which no one denies) that, to render His atonement valid *in actu secundo,* our Divine Saviour had first to assure Himself of its acceptation on the part of God, not indeed *per modum principii dignificantis,* but *per modum conditionis praeviae.* This is beside the question. What the Scotists assert is that the satisfaction which Christ made for our sins was intrinsically insufficient or inadequate, and that what it lacked in intrinsic merit was supplied by God's extrinsic acceptation. Their basic error consists in this that they fail to distinguish between the physical entity and the ethical value of Christ's meritorious actions, confounding the finite character of the former with the infinity of the latter. Justly, therefore, do the Thomists [10]

10 Cfr. Billuart, *De Incarn.,* diss. 19, art. 5.

insist that the Hypostatic Union endows a physically finite act with a morally infinite value, because it is the infinite Divine Person that performs that act as *principium quod,* employing the finite nature merely as *principium quo.* Were we to trace the Scotist theory to its sources, we should probably find that its originators had no clear conception of the character of theandric operation and misconceived the true nature and scope of the Hypostatic Union.[11]

Thesis II: The satisfaction which Christ made for our sins was not only adequate, but rigorous, according to the standard of strict justice.

Proof. In the preceding thesis we saw that Christ's vicarious atonement was quantitatively adequate, *i. e.,* equivalent to all the sins of mankind. We have now to show that it was adequate also in quality, *i. e.,* measured by the standard of strict justice (*secundum rigorem iustitiae*).

In other words, it was not necessary for God's mercy to supply anything over and above the satisfaction rendered by Christ, since this satisfaction fully covered all just claims.

This thesis does not embody an article of faith. It is not even a theological conclusion. But it voices the

11 On the uncertain teaching of Scotus cfr. P. Minges, O. F. M., *Compend. Theol. Dogmat. Specialis,* Vol. I, pp. 213 sqq., Monachii 1901; *Theologische Quartalschrift,* Tübingen, 1907, pp. 241 sqq. On the general subject of this thesis cfr. also De Lugo, *De Myst. Incarn.,* disp. 6, sect. 1; Scheeben, *Dogmatik,* Vol. III, §251, Freiburg 1882.

more general teaching of Catholic divines, especially of the Thomist school, and of Suarez, Tanner, Gregory of Valentia, Franzelin, and others. In a limited way we may also number among its defenders those Scotist theologians who, like Mastrius, admit that the atonement satisfied divine justice, though not to its full extent.

a) It pertains to the dogmatic treatise *De Deo Uno* [12] to show that the only kind of relation possible between God and His creatures is a free but real relation of rights and duties based upon the veracity and fidelity of the Creator. Christ's vicarious atonement embodies all the conditions necessary and sufficient to establish a relation of strict and rigorous justice. These conditions are five in number, to wit: (α) Equivalence of debit and credit; (β) difference of person between debtor and creditor; (γ) payment of the debt out of the debtor's own means; (δ) absence of all other indebtedness; (ε) payment of the debt in person or through a bondsman. These conditions are selected somewhat arbitrarily, and it is not easy to prove that Christ fulfilled them all. For this reason some theologians prefer not to speak of a *rigor iustitiae*. However, the *sententia communior* rests on fairly solid ground.

α) That Christ fulfilled the first of the conditions enumerated was shown in Thesis I.

β) Condition number two demands that debtor and

12 Cfr. Pohle-Preuss, *God: His Knowability, Essence and Attributes*, pp. 457 sqq.

creditor must be separate and distinct persons. "*Satisfactio debet esse ad alterum.*" No one can be his own debtor. How could Christ fulfil this condition? Since He is Himself God, is it not physically the same person that merits and rewards? This difficulty cannot be solved by the retort that Christ renders satisfaction to God the Father. Humanity's creditor was not the Father alone, but the whole Trinity.[13] The right solution seems to be this: In atoning for our sins, Christ acts both as man and as God, and hence makes satisfaction virtually as a double person: (1) the man Jesus makes satisfaction to God for our sins in His human nature, as if He were a different person from the Logos; (2) The Logos, as God, accepts this satisfaction. If Christ, as man, was able to practice the virtues of obedience and worship towards Himself as God, it can be no contradiction to say that, as man, He gave satisfaction to Himself, *qua* God, according to the strict measure of justice.

We must, however, beware of misinterpreting the expression *duplex persona moralis,* as Berruyer (a pupil of Hardouin) did when he asserted that the humanity of our Lord was a *quasi-suppositum,* to which, as to a distinct human person, must be ascribed certain actions of Christ which had no intrinsic hypostatic connexion with the Person of the Logos.[14]

γ) The third of the conditions enumerated above is

13 "What does it mean to be the mediator between God and men?" asks St. Augustine, and answers the question as follows: "It means to be a mediator not between the Father and men, but between God and men. What is God? He is Father, Son, and Holy Ghost. . . . Christ was constituted mediator between this Trinity and the infirmity and iniquity of men." *Ennar. in Ps.*, 29, 2, 1.

14 On this dangerous error see Legrand, *De Incarn.*, diss. 11, Paris 1860; von Schäzler, *Das Dogma von der Menschwerdung Gottes,* §24, Freiburg 1870; Scheeben, *Dogmatik,* Vol. III, pp. 29 sqq., Freiburg 1882; B. Dörholt, *Die Lehre von der Genugtuung Christi,* pp. 435 sqq., Paderborn 1891.

that the debtor must pay his liability out of his own belongings. "*Satisfactio debet fieri ex bonis propriis.*" Did Christ fulfil this condition? As He was a man, His power of giving satisfaction for our sins (*vis merendi sive satisfaciendi*) must have been a grace, *i. e.*, a free gift of God, and consequently the atonement cannot have been a payment made by Him out of His own means. Even the supernatural merits of a justified man, being due to pure grace, cannot satisfy rigorous justice. Indeed we may broadly say that, as man possesses nothing of his own, but has received everything he has from God, whether by creation or by grace, so Christ's human nature, which was the *principium quo* of His meritorious and expiatory action, was not His own but a gift of the debtor, *i. e.*, God.

This objection may be met as follows: It was not the man Jesus, but the Godman, whose meritorious actions made satisfaction for our sins. In other words, not the human nature of Christ as such made satisfaction, but the Divine Logos through the functions of His human nature, which, by virtue of the Hypostatic Union, is so intimately united to the Logos that He possesses and governs it with absolute sovereignty as its sole *principium quod*. To attribute such a sovereign control over the human nature of Christ to the Father and the Holy Ghost, *i. e.*, to the Trinity *qua* Godhead, would be tantamount to asserting that it was not the Logos alone who was made flesh, but the whole Blessed Trinity.[15] But this is manifestly repugnant. The human nature of Christ was the personal property of the Logos, and the satisfaction He made through that nature was made *ex bonis propriis*.[16]

δ) We come to the fourth condition: "*Satisfactio*

15 Cfr. Pohle-Preuss, *Christology*, pp. 132 sqq.

16 Cfr. Ysambert, *De Myst. Incarn.*, disp. 6, art. 2–3, Paris 1639.

debet esse ex alias indebitis." Satisfaction must be made by means of something which the debtor does not already owe to his creditor on some other account. It may be argued that this condition, too, remained unfulfilled in the case of our Divine Saviour, because whatever He did and suffered, He was obliged to do and suffer for reasons other than that prompting the atonement, such as gratitude and obedience to God, a feeling of dependence, piety, etc. Can an action to which one is obliged by so many titles be in strict justice regarded as meritorious?

Suarez offers two solutions of this difficulty. (1) The *rigor iustitiae,* he says, is to be measured purely and solely by the *titulus iustitiae.* Even if a debtor were obligated by gratitude towards his creditor, he would nevertheless satisfy rigorous justice as soon as he paid the last farthing of his indebtedness. Though other duties remained, justice as such would be satisfied. (2) The intrinsic merit of the satisfaction which Christ made for our sins is infinite, and as such capable of satisfying, not merely one single title of justice, but many, nay, an infinite number of such titles. Consequently justice can be rigorously satisfied even though there are other titles and duties.

ε) The last condition is that satisfaction must be made by the debtor for himself. *"Satisfactio debet fieri pro se ipso, non pro alienis."* Strictly speaking, Christ did not fulfil this condition, because He made atonement for others. It is to be noted, however, that the *rigor iustitiae* can be satisfied by proxy, provided the substitute is formally accepted by the creditor and the proportion between debt and reparation is strictly observed. Let it not be objected that where an offence has been committed the offended person waives his claim to strict justice by surrendering his right to personal satisfaction. He does not remit the debt, nor any part thereof, but merely commutes it into something of equal value.[17]

Thesis III: The satisfaction which Christ made for our sins was more than adequate and rigorous; it was superabundant.

This thesis may be characterized as "*communis,*" since it is held by practically all theological schools.

Proof. a) A Scriptural argument may be drawn from St. Paul's antithetical sentences in tracing the analogy between Adam and Christ. Cfr. Rom. V, 15: "But not as the offence, so also the gift. For if by the offence of one many died; much more[18] the grace of God, and the gift, by the grace of one man, Jesus Christ, hath abounded unto many."[19] And even more pointedly Rom. V, 20: "Where sin abounded,[20] grace did more abound."[21] The Apostle here distinctly asserts that Christ gave superabundant satisfaction for our sins. The sin was great, but the atonement and the graces flowing therefrom are still greater.[22]

17 Cfr. on the subject of these conditions and their fulfilment by Christ: Franzelin, *De Verbo Incarn.*, thes. 47, Rome 1881 (new edition, 1910); B. Dörholt, *Die Lehre von der Genugtuung Christi*, pp. 424 sqq., Paderborn 1891; Tepe, *Inst. Theol.*, Vol. III, pp. 639 sqq., Paris 1896.

18 *Multo magis*, πολλῷ μᾶλλον.

19 *In plures abundavit*, εἰς τοὺς πολλοὺς ἐπερίσσευσεν.

20 *Abundavit*, ἐπλεόνασεν.

21 *Superabundavit gratia*, ὑπερεπερίσσευσεν ἡ χάρις.

22 Cfr. Eph. I, 3-8; John X, 10.

b) The Fathers generally held that the adequacy of the atonement can be most effectively demonstrated from its superabundant meritoriousness.

Thus St. Cyril of Jerusalem trenchantly argues: "He who died for us was of no less value. He was not a visible lamb, no mere man, nor yet an angel, but the incarnate God. The wickedness of sinners was not as great as the righteousness of Him who died for us. Our sins were not equal to the justice of Him who died for us."[23] St. Chrysostom exemplifies this truth as follows: "Our experience has been like that of a man who was cast into prison with his wife and children and servants for a debt of ten oboli, and another man came and plumped down not only ten oboli, but ten thousand gold talents, and then led the prisoner into the royal chamber, placed him on an exalted throne, and allowed him to share in the highest honors. . . . For Christ paid far more than we owed, and in a larger measure, like as the infinite ocean exceeds in magnitude a tiny drop of water."[24]

c) If Christ's vicarious atonement was superabundantly meritorious, that is to say, far in excess of the sins for which it was made, its intrinsic worth must have been actually infinite. This inference is demanded by all the rules of theological logic, and hence we need not wonder that Suarez lays it down as the common teaching of

23 *Catech.*, 33, c. 13.

24 *Hom. in Ep. ad Rom.*, 10, 2. Additional Patristic texts *apud* Petav., XII, 9 and Thomassin, IX, 9. Cfr. also B. Dörholt, *Die Lehre von der Genugtuung Christi*, pp. 376 sqq., 419 sqq.; Muth, *Die Heilstat Christi*, pp. 228 sqq.

Catholic divines that "the actions of Christ possessed a value which was absolutely and strictly infinite in making satisfaction and acquiring merits before God." [25]

a) St. Thomas demonstrates this proposition by a theological argument based on the infinite dignity of the Godman. "The dignity of Christ's flesh," he says, "must not be estimated solely by the nature of the flesh, but by the assuming person; it was the flesh of God, hence its dignity is infinite." [26] As a matter of fact, the intrinsic moral value of an action varies in proportion to the dignity of him who performs it, and therefore the actions of a person of infinite dignity, when offered in satisfaction for an offence, must be infinitely meritorious.

To demonstrate the infinite value of Christ's vicarious atonement, it is not necessary to have recourse to its superabundant merit; the proposition follows as a corollary from the fact of its mere adequacy. If no one but a Godman was able to give adequate satisfaction for our sins, each and every one of Christ's theandric actions, even the most insignificant, must have been sufficient, nay more than sufficient, for the purposes of the atonement, because each and every action performed by a Godman is by its very nature infinitely meritorious.

As to the question, why the meritorious actions of our Lord had of necessity to culminate in His dolorous passion and death, St. Thomas says: "If we regard the *amount* paid for the redemption of the human race, any suffering undergone by Christ, even without death, would

25 *"Opera Christi Domini habuisse valorem absolute et simpliciter infinitum ad satisfaciendum et merendum apud Deum."* *De Incarn.*, disp. 4, sect. 4, n. 3.—On the untenableness of the Scotistic theory of extrinsic acceptation v. *supra*, pp. 63 sqq.

26 *S. Theol.*, 3a, qu. 48, art. 2, ad 3. Cfr. Suarez, *op. cit.*, n. 17 sqq.

have sufficed for the redemption of the human race, on account of the infinite dignity of His person. . . . But if we regard the *payment* of the price, it must be observed that no other suffering less than Christ's death was deemed sufficient by God the Father and by Christ Himself to redeem the human race." [27]

β) That the satisfaction which Christ made for our sins was infinite, may also be inferred from certain utterances (though they are not ex-cathedra decisions) of the Holy See. Among the propositions of Bajus condemned by Pope Pius V in the year 1567 is the following: "The works of justice and temperance performed by Christ derived no additional value from the dignity of His person." [28] Hence it is Catholic teaching that the actions of Christ derived a higher value from the "dignity of His Person." How high is this value to be rated? Evidently it must have corresponded to the infinite dignity of the Godman,—which is merely another way of saying that it was infinite.

A far more important pronouncement for our present purpose is this from the Bull *"Unigeni-*

27 *"Si ergo loquamur de redemptione humani generis quantum ad quantitatem pretii, sic quaelibet passio Christi etiam sine morte suffecisset ad redemptionem humani generis propter infinitam dignitatem personae . . . Si autem loquamur quantum ad deputationem pretii, sic dicendum est quod non sunt deputatae ad redemptionem humani generis a Deo Patre et Christo aliae passiones Christi absque morte." Quodlib.* 2, art 2.—Cfr. Dörholt, *op. cit.*, pp. 405 sqq.

28 *"Opera iustitiae et temperantiae, quas Christus fecit, ex dignitate personae operantis non traxerunt maiorem valorem."* Prop. 19 (Denzinger-Bannwart, *Enchiridion,* n. 1019).

tus" of Pope Clement VI, A. D. 1343: "He is known to have shed, not a little drop of blood,—though this would have sufficed for the redemption of the entire human race, because of the [Hypostatic] Union with the Logos,—but streams of it, like unto a river. . . . That the mercy involved in such a large effusion [of blood] be not rendered vain, empty, and superfluous, He laid up for the Church militant a copious treasure, which the good Father desires to dispense to his children, in order that it may become an infinite store-house for men, and that those who make use of it may share in the friendship of God."[29] Pope Clement, in issuing his Bull, did not intend to define the dogmatic teaching of the Church with regard to this "infinite treasure." Nor does the document contain any clear expression as to whether Christ's merits are to be conceived as actually or potentially infinite. Hence the above-quoted words cannot be said to constitute a binding dogmatic definition. We may, however, safely assume that Clement VI intended to represent the treasure of Christ's merits as actually infinite, for this is the obvious meaning of his words, considered both in

29 "*Non guttam sanguinis modicam, quae tamen propter unionem ad Verbum pro redemptione totius humani generis suffecisset, sed copiose velut quoddam profluvium noscitur effudisse . . . Quantum ergo exinde, ut nec supervacua, inanis et superflua tantae effusionis miseratio redderetur, thesaurum militanti Ecclesiae acquisivit, volens suis thesaurizare filiis pius Pater, ut sic sit infinitus thesaurus hominibus, quo qui usi sunt Dei amicitiae participes sunt effecti.*" Denzinger Bannwart, *Enchiridion*, n. 550.

themselves and in connection with the context.

The doctrine of the superabundant merits of Jesus Christ and His Saints forms the groundwork of the Catholic teaching on indulgences, which we shall explain more fully in a later volume of this series.[30]

ARTICLE 2

EXTRINSIC PERFECTION OR UNIVERSALITY OF THE ATONEMENT

If, as we have shown in the preceding Article, the satisfaction made for our sins by Christ was intrinsically perfect, there is *a priori* ground for assuming that it must have embraced all men without exception. In matter of fact the universality of the atonement objectively coincides with the universality of God's will to save the entire human race (*voluntas salvifica*), Here we shall merely touch upon a few important points bearing on the Redemption.

Thesis I: Christ died for all the faithful, not only for the predestined.

This proposition is strictly *de fide*.

Proof. The predestined are those who actually attain to eternal salvation. Of the "faithful," *i. e.*, those who have the true faith, many are unfortunately lost.

a) Predestinarianism was taught by Calvin, and also by the younger Jansenius, who hereti-

30 In connection with the Sacrament of Penance.

cally asserted that "It savours of Semi-Pelagianism to say that Christ died, or shed His blood, for all men without exception." [1] This proposition was censured as "false, foolhardy, and scandalous" by Innocent X, who added that, "understood in the sense that Christ died for the salvation of the predestined only," Jansenius' thesis is furthermore "impious, blasphemous . . . and heretical." Consequently it must be accepted as an article of faith that Christ died also for those who were not predestined. These are the "faithful," *i. e.* (in the New Testament) all who have received the Sacrament of Baptism, be they infants or adults. For all baptized Christians are bound to accept the Creed, which says that Christ "descended from Heaven for us men and for our salvation." [2]

b) Sacred Scripture is so clear on this point that we may well marvel at the existence of Predestinarianism. St. Paul must have had the "faithful" in mind when he wrote to the Thessalonians: "For God hath not appointed us unto wrath, but unto the purchasing of salvation by our Lord Jesus Christ, who died for us." [3] Again, Christ Himself, assuredly the most faith-

1 *"Semipelagianum est dicere, Christum pro omnibus omnino hominibus mortuum esse aut sanguinem fudisse." Prop. Damn. Iansenii,* 5 (Denzinger-Bannwart, *Enchiridion,* n. 1096).

2 *". . . qui propter nos homines et propter nostram salutem descendit de coelis."*

3 1 Thess. V, 9 sq.

ful exponent of the Divine Will, in the touching prayer which He pronounced as the High Priest of humanity, included all the faithful,—in fact, indirectly, the whole human race. Cfr. John XVII, 20 sq.: *"Non pro eis [scil. Apostolis] autem rogo tantum, sed et pro eis qui credituri sunt*[4] *per verbum eorum in me, . . . ut credat mundus,*[5] *quia tu me misisti* — And not for them [*i. e.,* the Apostles] only do I pray, but for them also who through their word shall believe in me; . . . that the world may believe that thou hast sent me."

c) The teaching of the Fathers on this point is copiously expounded by Petavius,[6] and we need not expatiate on it here.[7]

Thesis II: Christ died for all men without exception.

This thesis may be qualified as *"saltem fidei proxima."*

Proof. The Provincial Council of Quiercy (A. D. 853) defined against Gottschalk: "As there never was, is or will be any man whose nature was not assumed by our Lord Jesus Christ, so there never was, is or will be any man for whom He has not suffered; though not all

4 περὶ τῶν πιστευόντων.

5 ἵνα ὁ κόσμος πιστεύσῃ.

6 *De Incarn.*, XIII, 2 sq.

7 On the misrepresentation of St. Augustine's teaching by the Jansenists consult Dechamps, *De Haeresi Janseniana*, l. II, disp. 7.

are redeemed by the mystery of His passion."[8] Pope Alexander VIII, A. D. 1690, formally condemned the proposition that "Christ gave Himself for us as an oblation to God, not for the elect only, but for all the faithful, and for the faithful alone."[9] The Tridentine Council defines the dogmatic teaching of the Church on this point as follows: "Him [Christ] God hath proposed as a propitiator, through faith in His blood, for our sins; and not for our sins only, but also for those of the whole world."[10]

a) This Tridentine teaching is thoroughly Scriptural, in fact it is couched in the very language of Holy Writ. Cfr. 1 John II, 2: *"Et ipse est propitiatio*[11] *pro peccatis nostris, non pro nostris autem tantum, sed etiam pro totius mundi*[12]— He is the propitiation for our sins: and not for ours only, but also for those of the whole world." 1 Tim. II, 6 must be interpreted in consonance with the text just quoted. *"Qui*

8 *"Christus Iesus D. N., sicut nullus homo est, fuit vel erit, cuius natura in illo assumpta non fuerit, ita nullus est, fuit vel erit homo, pro quo passus non fuerit, licet non omnes passionis eius mysterio redimantur."* The controversies incident to the Council of Valence (A. D. 855) were due to a misunderstanding. Cfr. B. Dörholt, *Die Lehre von der Genugtuung Christi,* pp. 323 sqq.

9 *". . . dedit semetipsum pro nobis oblationem Deo, non pro solis electis, sed pro omnibus et solis fidelibus."* (Denzinger-Bannwart, *Enchiridion,* n. 1294.)

10 *"Hunc proposuit Deus propitiatorem per fidem in sanguine ipsius pro peccatis nostris, non solum autem pro nostris, sed etiam pro totius mundi." Conc. Trid.,* Sess. VI, cap. 2 (Denzinger-Bannwart, n. 794).

11 ἱλασμός.

12 ἀλλὰ καὶ περὶ ὅλου τοῦ κόσμου.

dedit redemptionem semetipsum pro omnibus [*scil. hominibus*] —Who gave himself a redemption for all [*i. e.,* for all men]." The context shows that St. Paul means to emphasize the universality of God's will to save all men. We may also point in confirmation of our thesis to such passages as 2 Cor. V, 14, in which the Apostle numbers among the elect such as are still in the state of original sin as well as those who are justified. "*Si unus pro omnibus*[13] *mortuus est, ergo omnes*[14] *mortui sunt* — If one died for all, then all are dead."[15]

b) The Jansenists did not deny that the Fathers who wrote before Pelagius clearly taught the vicarious atonement to be as universal as God's will to save mankind, *i. e.,* that it embraces all human beings without exception. But they claimed that a change came with St. Augustine, who succumbed to the evil influence of Predestinarianism. It is to be noted that the famous African Doctor was warmly defended against this calumnious charge by one of his contemporaneous disciples, St. Prosper of Aquitaine.[16]

13 ὑπὲρ πάντων.

14 οἱ πάντες.

15 For an explanation of this text see Al. Schäfer, *Erklärung der beiden Briefe an die Korinther,* pp. 439 sqq., Münster 1903.

16 We cannot enter into the controversy here. The student will find it exhaustively treated by Dörholt, *Lehre von der Genugtuung Christi,* Paderborn 1896, pp. 317 sqq., by Tricassin, *De Praedestinatione,* p. I, sect. 7, punct. 4 sqq., and by Franzelin, *De Deo Uno,* thes. 32, Rome 1883. The fate of unbaptized infants will be discussed in Vol. VII of this series.

Thesis III: The atonement did not benefit the fallen angels.

This proposition is *de fide*.

Proof. Origen taught that Christ also died for the demons, who were destined at some future time to be released from hell. This error (ἀποκατάστασις πάντων) was closely related to another, harbored by the same learned but erratic divine, *viz.*: that the Logos assumed the form of an angel to redeem the lost angels, just as He became man to redeem sinful humanity. These vagaries were condemned as heretical by a council held at Constantinople in 543, and again by the Fifth Ecumenical Council, A. D. 553.[17]

The dogma embodied in our present thesis is intimately bound up with that concerning the fall of the angels and their eternal banishment from Paradise.[18] Being condemned to everlasting hell-fire, the evil spirits can have no share in the merits of the Redeemer. "For although there is assigned to angels also perdition in the fire prepared for the Devil and his angels," says Tertullian, "yet a restoration was never promised

17 Cfr. Denzinger, *Enchiridion*, ed. 9, n. 193 and 198. Fr. Diekamp (*Die origenistischen Streitigkeiten im 6. Jahrhundert und das V. allgemeine Konzil*, Münster 1899) has put a quietus on an ancient controversy by showing that Origenism was condemned both by the Council of Constantinople in 543 and by the Fifth General Council in 553, though the *acta* of the latter do not mention the fact. Cfr. Chr. Pesch, S. J., *Theologische Zeitfragen*, Vol. II, Freiburg 1901.

18 Cfr. Pohle-Preuss, *God the Author of Nature and the Supernatural*, pp. 340 sqq.

them. No charge about the salvation of angels did Christ ever receive from the Father; and that which the Father neither promised nor commanded, Christ could not have undertaken." [19]

Thesis IV: The doctrine of the universality of the atonement is not disproved by the fact that many human beings are eternally lost.

This proposition may be qualified as theologically certain.

Proof. The Council of Trent teaches: "But, though He died for all, yet not all receive the benefit of His death, but those only unto whom the merit of His Passion is communicated." [20]

According to Holy Scripture, the universality of Christ's vicarious atonement is not absolute but conditional. Those only are saved who comply with the conditions necessary for participating in the fruits of the Redemption, *viz.:* baptism, faith, contrition, coöperation with grace, perseverance. Cfr. Mark XVI, 16: "*Qui crediderit et baptizatus fuerit, salvus erit; qui vero non crediderit, condemnabitur* — He that believeth and is baptized, shall be saved; but he that believeth not shall be condemned."

19 *De Carne Christi,* c. 14.—Cfr. Dörholt, *Lehre von der Genugtuung Christi,* pp. 353 sqq.—On the participation of the good angels in the merits of the Redeemer see Pohle-Preuss, *Christology,* pp. 243 sqq.

20 "*Verum etsi ille pro omnibus mortuus est, non omnes tamen eius beneficium recipiunt, sed ii dumtaxat, quibus meritum passionis communicatur.*" Sess. VI, cap. 3. Denzinger-Bannwart, n. 795.

"The blood of thy Lord," observes St. Augustine, "is given for thee, if thou wilt; if thou wilt not, it is not given for thee." [21]

Theologians distinguish between God's antecedent and His consequent will to save men. Antecedently He willed to save all men without exception, even those who are lost; *voluntate consequenti*, however, the damned are in fact, though not in principle, excluded from the fruits of the Redemption. It is correct to say, however, in spite of this limitation, that Christ also died for the damned, both past and future, because they are lost through their own fault.

The atonement may be regarded as universal from still another point of view. Satisfaction is either merely sufficient or efficacious. It is sufficient if it provides adequate means of salvation. It is efficacious if these means are appropriated and utilized by those to whom they are offered. Catholic divines unanimously teach that Christ died for all men *secundum sufficientiam, non tamen secundum efficaciam*. It is indeed quite obvious that if a man neglects to appropriate the fruits of the Redemption, he derives no more benefit therefrom than one who is dying of thirst receives from a spring within his reach but from which he refuses to drink. "Although [Christ] by His death made sufficient satisfaction for the sins of the human race," says St. Thomas, "yet each individual man must seek for the remedies whereby to work out his own salvation. The death of Christ may in a manner be called the universal cause of salvation, like as the sin of the first man was, after a fashion, the universal cause of damnation. But it is necessary that the universal cause be applied to each one

21 *Serm.*, 344, n. 4.

in particular, that each may participate in its effect. The effect of the sin of our first parents descends to each one of us by the propagation of the flesh, while the effect of our Saviour's death comes to each by spiritual regeneration . . . and therefore it is necessary that each individual human being should seek to be regenerated through Christ and to employ all other means whereby the death of Christ becomes efficacious." [22] In other words, the atonement is universal only with regard to its objective value or sufficiency, not in respect of its subjective application or efficaciousness. [23]

22 "*Quamvis autem sufficienter pro peccatis humani generis suâ morte satisfecerit, sunt tamen unicuique remedia propriae salutis quaerenda. Mors enim Christi est quasi quaedam universalis causa salutis, sicut peccatum primi hominis fuit quasi universalis causa damnationis. Oportet autem universalem causam applicari ad unumquodque specialiter, ut effectum universalis causae participet. Effectus igitur peccati primi parentis pervenit ad unumquemque per carnis originem, effectus autem mortis Christi pertingit ad unumquemque per spiritualem regenerationem . . . et ideo oportet quod unusquisque quaerat regenerari per Christum et alia suscipere, in quibus virtus mortis Christi operatur.*" *Contra Gent.*, IV, 55, *sub fin.*

23 Cfr. Dörholt, *op. cit.*, pp. 307 sqq., 330 sqq.

SECTION 3

THE CONCRETE REALIZATION OF CHRIST'S VICARIOUS ATONEMENT

In the two preceding Sections we have shown that the atonement was real and intrinsically as well as extrinsically perfect. The question now arises: What were the specific actions by which the Godman made satisfaction for our sins? Or, to express it in simpler terms, How did Christ redeem us? We pray: "By Thy holy Cross Thou hast redeemed the world." This does not imply that our Divine Saviour's previous actions had no reference to the purpose of the Redemption. His whole life, from His conception to His death on the Cross, was a chain of expiatory actions, each in itself sufficient to redeem the world *in actu primo*. But it was an essential feature of the scheme of salvation that *in actu secundo, i. e.,* actually, no satisfaction was acceptable but that which had its consummation in the tragedy on Golgotha.

In the present Section, therefore, we shall first treat of Christ's Death on the Cross (Article 1) and then of two subsequent events of peculiar soteriological import, *viz.:* His Descent into Hell (Article 2) and His Glorious Resurrection (Article 3).

ARTICLE 1

CHRIST'S DEATH ON THE CROSS

We are here considering the death of our Divine Redeemer not as a sacrifice, but merely as the means of our salvation. It was by His passion and death that Jesus actually redeemed mankind. The circumstance that His death was a bloody sacrifice constitutes Him a priest; this aspect of the matter will receive due attention in Part II, Chapter 1, *infra*.

1. CHRIST'S DEATH THE EFFICIENT CAUSE OF OUR REDEMPTION.—In view of the central position which the Cross of Christ occupies in the history of the Redemption, the Tridentine Council asserted a truth self-evident to every Christian when it defined: "Of this justification the causes are these: the final cause indeed is the glory of God and of Jesus Christ, . . . while the efficient cause is a merciful God; . . . but the meritorious cause is His most beloved only-begotten Son, our Lord Jesus Christ, who . . . merited justification for us by His most holy Passion on the wood of the Cross and made satisfaction for us to God the Father." [1]

1 "*Huius iustificationis causae sunt finalis quidem gloria Dei et Christi, . . . efficiens vero misericors Deus, . . . meritoria autem dilectissimus Unigenitus suus D. N. Iesus Christus, qui . . . suâ sanctissimâ passione in ligno crucis nobis iustificationem meruit et pro nobis Deo Patri* [*scil. per appropriationem*] *satisfecit.*" *Conc. Trid.*,

So important a dogma must loom large in the New Testament and be at least foreshadowed in the Old.

a) Apart from certain Old Testament types (such as the sacrifice of Isaac, the scapegoat, the brazen serpent, etc.),[2] the Messianic prophecies afford numerous intimations of the bloody passion and death of the future Messias. Most of these occur in the prophecies of Isaias and the Book of Psalms. Isaias, in speaking of the satisfaction rendered by the "servant of the Lord," [3] invariably describes it as a dolorous passion followed by death.[4] The 21st Psalm characterizes salvation as the outcome of intense tribulation and suffering. "But I am a worm, and no man; the reproach of men, and the outcast of the people. All they that saw me have laughed me to scorn: they have spoken with the lips, and wagged the head. . . . My strength is dried up like a potsherd, and my tongue hath cleaved to my jaws: and thou hast brought me down into the dust of death. . . . They have dug my hands and feet. They have numbered all my bones. And they have looked and stared upon me. They parted my garments amongst them; and upon my vesture they cast lots." [5]

Sess. VI, cap. 7 (Denzinger-Bannwart, n. 799).

2 On these and other types of the suffering Messias see A. J. Maas, S. J., *Christ in Type and Prophecy*, Vol. II, pp. 322–343.

3 Is. XLII, 1–9; XLIX, 1 sqq.; L, 4 sqq., LIII, 4 sqq. Cfr. Maas, *op. cit.*, Vol. II, pp. 231 sqq.

4 See *supra*, pp. 46 sq.

5 Ps. XXI, 7 sqq. Cfr. Maas, *op. cit.*, Vol. II, pp. 264–287.

b) The New Testament fairly swarms with passages in support of the dogma. Christ Himself says: *"Filius hominis non venit ministrari, sed ministrare, et dare animam suam redemptionem*[6] *pro multis* — The Son of man is not come to be ministered unto, but to minister, and to give his life a redemption for many."[7] And again: *"Sic enim Deus dilexit mundum, ut Filium suum unigenitum daret,*[8] *ut omnis qui credit in eum, non pereat, sed habeat vitam aeternam* — God so loved the world, as to give his only begotten Son; that whosoever believeth in him, may not perish, but may have life everlasting."[9] St. Paul attests the same truth in somewhat different terms. *"Qui etiam proprio Filio suo non pepercit,"* he says, *"sed pro nobis omnibus tradidit*[10] *illum* — He spared not even his own Son, but delivered him up for us all."[11] The notion that Christ died for us on the Cross assumes concrete form in the shedding of His blood "unto the remission of sins."[12] Hence the well-known Pauline axiom, *"Sine sanguinis effusione non fit remissio*[13]— Without shedding of blood there is no remission."[14] Therefore, too, subjective salvation, *i. e.,* the application of

6 λύτρον = ransom.

7 Matth. XX, 28.

8 ἔδωκεν.

9 John III, 16.

10 παρέδωκεν.

11 Rom. VIII, 32.

12 Cfr. Matth. XXVI, 28.

13 καὶ χωρὶς αἱματεκχυσίας οὐ γίνεται ἄφεσις.

14 Heb. IX, 22.

the fruits of the Redemption to the individual soul, is described as "the sprinkling of the blood of Jesus Christ,"[15] and the Redemption was not "consummated" until Christ gave up the ghost.[16]

2. THE CONGRUITY OF CHRIST'S DEATH ON THE CROSS.—It was fitting that Christ should die for us on the Cross. The reasons are admirably developed by St. Thomas.[17] We must confine ourselves to a summary of the most important of them.

a) It would have been unbecoming for the Redeemer to die of old age or disease,[18] or to fall beneath the blows of an assassin. His high office as Saviour of the human race demanded that He should die a public death. In no other way could He have so effectively sealed the truth of His teaching. Nothing could have been more conducive to the spread of His Gospel than His bloody martyrdom, which contained within itself the proof of His teaching and power. The fact that He met death unflinchingly gained for Him a greater number of enthusiastic adherents than many years of teaching could have done. What is the poison cup that Socrates put to his lips in comparison with the agony suffered by Jesus Christ? His reward was proportionate to the magnitude of His suffering. This consideration (namely, that He merited His glorification by intense suffering) implies a profound teleology, which may be truly termed divine.

15 1 Pet. I, 2: "*aspersionem sanguinis Iesu Christi.*" Cfr. Heb. IX, 13 sq.

16 "*Consummatum est.*" John XIX, 30.—The Patristic argument is developed by Tepe, *Inst. Theol.*, Vol. III, pp. 651 sqq.

17 *S. Theol.*, 3a, qu. 46, art. 1–4, 11; qu. 47, art. 4; qu. 50, art. 1.

18 Cfr. Pohle-Preuss, *Christology*, pp. 81 sqq.

b) In regard to those for whom He gave up His life, Christ could not have selected a more congruous manner of dying than that which He actually chose. The path of Christian perfection runs between two poles — hatred of sin and the practice of virtue. From both points of view the cruel drama enacted on Golgotha was eminently effective. The power of sin could not be broken except by a strong opposing force. This may be regarded either objectively or subjectively.

α) The sin of our first parents had doomed the human race to spiritual death, a terrible penalty which entailed the death of the body.[19] Hence it was eminently proper that our Divine Redeemer should by His bodily death destroy the spell of spiritual death and thereby restore man to that corporeal immortality which had been one of the prerogatives of the human race in Paradise, but was forfeited by sin. There is a striking parallel also between the first sinner's desire to be like unto God and the self-humiliation of the Godman, between the "tree of knowledge" and the "wood of the Cross." The antithesis between Christ's passion and death on the one hand, and sin on the other, may be traced in detail. Thus the unholy trinity of vices which we have inherited from our first parents — concupiscence of the eyes, concupiscence of the flesh, and pride of life — received a tremendous blow by the bitter passion and death of our Saviour,— concupiscence of the eyes in the distribution of his garments, concupiscence of the flesh in His disrobing and scourging, and pride of life in the imposition of the thorny crown and the crucifixion.

β) Nothing could produce a more impressive idea of the hideousness of sin than the contemplation of the

19 Cfr. Rom. V, 7 sqq.

mangled and blood-stained body of our crucified Redeemer.[20] It is apt to soften the hardest of hearts. He who dares to offend God in plain view of the Cross is an atrocious villain, because, in the words of St. Paul, he does not shrink from "crucifying again . . . the Son of God and making him a mockery."[21] The height of contemplation and the heroic practice of virtue to which the medieval mystics attained by meditating on the cruel sufferings of our Divine Redeemer, have been and still are within the reach of all men. Like St. John many have found by experience that love kindles love. "In this is charity: not as though we had loved God, but because he hath first loved us, and sent his Son to be a propitiation for our sins."[22]

Our crucified Redeemer is, moreover, a living and attractive model of all virtue. How would it be possible for us poor weak mortals to be virtuous had we not His glorious example to encourage us? Is there anything a selfish, effeminate man dreads more than pain and death? Yet the Passion of Christ has deprived both of their sting. St. Teresa had no other desire than either to die or to suffer (*aut mori aut pati*). Death, too, so terrible to human nature, has lost its horrors. With the crucifix clasped in his hands and the name of the Redeemer on his lips, the pious Christian calmly commends his soul to the Heavenly Father. In the Cross there is salvation, the Cross is a haven of refuge.[23]

20 On the extensive and intensive magnitude of our Lord's suffering see Cfr. Pesch, *Prael. Dogmat.*, Vol. IV, pp. 267 sqq.; *A. Kluge, Das Seelenleiden des Welterlösers,* Mainz 1905.

21 Heb. VI, 6.

22 1 John IV, 10.

23 Cfr. the Roman Catechism, Part I, ch. 5, qu. 4, 14; Billuart, *De Myst. Christi,* diss. 9, art. 1, and Oswald, *Die Erlösung in Christo Jesu,* Vol. II, §5, Paderborn 1887.

ARTICLE 2

CHRIST'S DESCENT INTO HELL

The Oriental and the ancient Roman versions of the so-called Apostles' Creed do not mention Christ's Descent into hell. But the doctrine is contained in the Spanish, Gallic, and Aquilean recensions and in the symbol "*Quicunque*," wrongly attributed to St. Athanasius. Hence the *descensus ad inferos* is commonly regarded as an article of faith. The Fourth Lateran Council (A. D. 1215) teaches somewhat more explicitly: "He descended into hell, . . . but He descended in soul and arose in flesh, and ascended equally in both." [1]

Durandus contended that the soul of Christ descended into hell dynamically but not substantially. This opinion was censured as heretical by Suarez.[2] And justly so; for it can be effectively refuted from Sacred Scripture. The same is true of Calvin's absurd notion [3] that Christ before and after His agonizing death suffered the tortures of the damned.

The nature of the place into which our Lord descended has never been dogmatically defined,

1 "*Descendit ad infernos, . . . sed descendit in anima et resurrexit in carne: ascenditque pariter in utroque.*" Caput "*Firmiter.*" (Denzinger-Bannwart, *Enchiridion*, n. 429.)

2 *De Myst. Vitae Christi*, disp. 43, sect. 2, n. 7.

3 *Inst.*, II, 16, 10.

but it is theologically certain that it was the so-called *limbus patrum* (*sinus Abrahae*).

1. Proof of the Dogma from Sacred Scripture and Tradition.—The dogma of Christ's Descent into hell is clearly contained both in Sacred Scripture and Tradition.

a) Ps. XV, 10: "*Non derelinques animam meam in inferno,*[4] *nec dabis Sanctum tuum videre corruptionem* — Thou wilt not leave my soul in hell, nor wilt thou give thy holy one to see corruption." This text contains a convincing argument for our dogma, because St. Peter directly applies it to Christ: "*Providens* [*David*] *locutus est de resurrectione Christi, quia neque derelictus est in inferno neque caro eius vidit corruptionem* — Foreseeing this, he [David] spoke of the resurrection of Christ. For neither was he left in hell, neither did his flesh see corruption."[5] The Greek term which the Vulgate renders by *infernum* is ᾄδης. It cannot mean *grave,* as Beza contended, because the soul of Christ was not buried; nor can it mean *death* (which is Calvin's interpretation), because the soul of Christ did not die. It must refer to a locality where the soul of our Lord sojourned until it was reunited with His "uncorrupted flesh" at the Resurrection.[6]

4 τὴν ψυχὴν εἰς ᾄδου.

5 Acts II, 31. Cfr. Acts XIII, 35.

6 Cfr. Bellarmine, *De Christo,* IV, 6–12; Maas, *Christ in Type and Prophecy,* Vol. I, pp. 140 sqq.; Vol. II, pp. 358 sqq., esp. p. 372.

This interpretation is confirmed by the teaching of St. Paul in his Epistle to the Ephesians: "Now that he ascended, what is it, but because he also descended first into the lower parts of the earth?[7] He that descended is the same also that ascended above all the heavens, that he might fill all things."[8] Christ's ascension here can only mean His return to Heaven. Consequently, the word *descend,* in contradistinction to *ascend,* must here be understood in a local sense. This is rendered all the more probable by the fact that the phrase *inferiores partes terrae* cannot be applied to Christ's burial, and still less metaphorically to the Incarnation. For the rest, St. Peter, (in a somewhat obscure passage, it is true),[9] explicitly observes that the soul of Christ "preached[10] to those spirits that were in prison,"—hence it must have been substantially present in a particular place, *i. e.,* the limbo.

b) The Tradition in support of our dogma is as ancient as it is positive.

St. Irenæus says: "For three days He dwelt in the place where the dead were."[11] Tertullian mentions Christ's Descent into hell in several passages of his works. We shall quote but one. "Nor did He ascend into the heights of heaven before descending into the lower parts of the earth, that He might there make the patriarchs and prophets partakers of Himself."[12] St. Augustine speaks with the authority of both Scripture

7 *εἰς τὰ κατώτερα μέρη τῆς γῆς.*

8 Eph. IV, 9 sq.

9 1 Pet. III, 18 sqq.

10 *ἐκήρυξε, praedicavit.*

11 "*Nunc autem tribus diebus conversatus est, ubi erant mortui.*" *Adv. Haereses,* V, 31, 1; cfr. also *Adv. Haereses,* IV, 27, 2.

12 "*Nec ante ascendit in sublimiora coelorum, quam descendit in inferiora terrarum, ut illic patriarchas et prophetas compotes sui faceret.*" *De Anima,* c. 55; cfr. also c. 4, 7.

and Tradition when he says: "Who but an unbeliever would deny that Christ was in the nether world?"[13]

2. MEANING OF THE TERM "HELL."—*Infernum* (ᾅδης, κατώτατα, Hebrew, שְׁאוֹל) may designate either (a) hell in the strict sense of the term, *i. e.,* the abode of the reprobates (*gehenna*); or (b) a place of purification after death, commonly called purgatory (*purgatorium*); or (c) the biding place of children who have died unbaptized (*limbus infantium*); or (d) the abode of the just men who lived before the coming of Christ (*limbus patrum*). To which of these four places did Christ descend?

a) The soul of our Lord did not descend to the abode of the damned.

Calvin's blasphemous assertion that the soul of Christ, from the beginning of His sacred Passion in the Garden of Gethsemane to the Resurrection, dwelled in the abode of the damned, and there suffered the *poena damni,* is based on an untenable exaggeration of the notion of vicarious atonement.[14] It is *not* true, as Calvin held, that Christ's Descent into hell constituted the climax of the atonement. The atonement culminated on the Cross. ("*Consummatum est.*") Nor can we conceive of any reasonable motive why our Lord should have descended into the gehenna of the damned. The human beings confined in that awful dungeon were abso-

13 "*Quis ergo nisi infidelis negaverit fuisse apud inferos Christum?*" *Ep. 104 ad Evodium, c. 2, 3* (Migne, *P. L.,* XXXIII, 710).

14 Cfr. Bellarmine, *De Christo,* V, 8.

lutely irredeemable, even as the demons themselves.[15] Moreover, a personal sojourn in hell would have been repugnant to the dignity of the Godman. St. Augustine does not hesitate to stigmatize as heretical the proposition that "When Christ descended into hell, the unbelieving believed and all were set free."[16] The "triumph over hell" which the Church celebrates in her Easter hymns did not require the substantial presence there of our Lord's soul; it was accomplished by His virtual or dynamic presence, *i. e.*, the exercise of His divine power.

Certain ancient ecclesiastical writers[17] held that on the occasion of His Descent Christ rescued from eternal torture the souls of certain pious heathens, *e. g.*, Socrates and Plato. This theory does not contradict the dogma that the pains of hell are eternal, as Suarez contends; but it must nevertheless be rejected as unfounded; first, because without positive proof to the contrary we are not permitted to assume an exception, and secondly, because there is no ground whatever for the assumption that these pious heathens were condemned to hell rather than relegated to the *limbus patrum.*

b) There is another opinion, held by several reputable theologians, *viz.*, that the soul of Christ appeared personally in purgatory to console the poor souls and to admit them to the beatific vision.

We may let this pass as a "pious opinion," provided its defenders refrain from denying that Christ also descended into the *limbus patrum.* But even with this limitation we can hardly admit that the theory is based on sufficient

15 V. *supra,* Sect. 2, Art. 2, Thesis 4.

16 *"Descendente Christo ad inferos credidisse incredulos et omnes exinde liberatos." De Haer.,* 79.

17 *E. g.,* Clement of Alexandria and Origen.

evidence. Two weighty arguments speak against it. It is a fundamental law of divine justice that whoever neglects to render satisfaction in this life must inevitably suffer in the next (*satispassio*), and Sacred Scripture affords no warrant for assuming that an exception was made in this instance, say after the manner of a plenary indulgence in commemoration of the Redemption. On the other hand it is highly improbable that all the inmates of purgatory should have finished the process of purification at exactly the same moment. In view of these considerations St. Thomas holds that the (merely virtual) presence of our Lord in purgatory resulted in nothing more than giving to the poor souls temporarily imprisoned there "the hope of an early beatitude." [18] The only exception the Angelic Doctor is disposed to make is in favor of those "who were already sufficiently purged, or who during their lifetime had by faith and devotion to the death of Christ merited the favor of being released from the temporal sufferings of purgatory on the occasion of His descent." [19]

c) Was it perhaps the *limbus puerorum, i. e.*, the abode of children who die in the state of original sin, into which our Saviour descended? It is difficult to see for what reason He should have gone there.

He could not benefit the souls of these children, because they have once for all arrived at their destination.

18 *S. Theol.*, 3a, qu 51, art. 3: *"Illis vero, qui detinebantur in purgatorio, spem gloriae consequendae dedit."*

19 *". . . qui iam sufficienter purgati erant, vel etiam qui, dum adhuc viverent, meruerunt per fidem et devotionem ad mortem Christi, ut eo descendente liberarentur a temporali purgatorii poena."* (*Ibid.*) Cfr. Billuart, *De Myst. Christi*, diss. 11, art. 3.

Nor can He have desired to triumph over them, because the fact that they are deprived of the beatific vision is not due to any malice on their part, but simply and solely to original sin contracted by their descent from Adam. As these infants are absolutely irredeemable in virtue of Christ's *voluntas salvifica consequens,*[20] we cannot even assume the existence of a special privilege in their favor. That which is impossible cannot be made the subject-matter of a privilege, not even at so solemn a juncture as the death of our Saviour.[21] Their fate does not involve cruelty nor injustice on the part of God, because, though deprived of the beatific vision, they enjoy a certain measure of natural happiness.[22]

d) Consequently, the only place to which the soul of Christ can have descended during the triduum intervening between His death and the Resurrection, is the *limbus patrum,* sometimes also called "bosom of Abraham."

The *limbus patrum* was the place in which the patriarchs and just men of the Old Testament, together with those heathens who had died in the state of grace, after having been cleansed from all stain of sin in purgatory, dwelled in the expectation of the beatific vision. That such a place existed we conclude from Heb. IX, 8: "The way into the holies [*i. e.,* Heaven] [23] was not yet

20 V. *supra,* Sect. 2, Art. 2, Thesis 4.

21 Cfr. St. Thomas, *S. Theol.,* 3a, qu. 52, art. 7: *"Pueri autem, qui cum originali peccato decesserant, nullo modo fuerant coniuncti passioni Christi per fidem et dilectionem. Neque enim fidem propriam habere potuerant, quia non habuerunt usum liberi arbitrii, neque per fidem parentum aut per aliquod fidei sacramentum* [*scil. baptismum*] *fuerant a peccato originali mundati. Et ideo descensus Christi ad inferos huiusmodi pueros non liberavit ab inferno."*

22 Cfr. Pohle-Preuss, *God the Author of Nature and the Supernatural,* pp. 300 sqq.

23 Cfr. Heb. X, 19.

made manifest, whilst the former tabernacle [*i. e.,* the Old Testament] was yet standing." We may also infer the (former) existence of such a place from the fact that Holy Scripture adverts to a state of imprisonment as an intermediary stage on the way to Heaven.

3. SPECULATIONS REGARDING THE LOCATION OF THE LIMBO.— The word limbo, which is derived from *limbus,* properly signifies *edge* or *border.* It owes its use as a technical term in theology to the ancient belief that the abode of the patriarchs was situated on the confines of hell, somewhere near the surface of the earth. Dante and Milton place the limbo at the outermost circle of hell.[24] Since the geocentric has been supplanted by the Copernican world-view, we know that the ancient notions of "above" and "below" are purely relative. Hence the traditional view with regard to the site of hell and the limbo does not appertain to the substance of dogma. The meagre data furnished by Revelation do not enable us to draw up a topographical map of the nether world. We know no more about the whereabouts of hell than we know about the location of what was once the limbo of the Fathers. The theological arguments of certain Scholastic writers, based on the geocentric conception of the universe, can claim no probability, much less certitude.[25]

24 Milton, *Paradise Lost,* III, 440 sqq.

25 On the limbo see P. J. Toner in the *Catholic Encyclopedia,* Vol.

4. THE SOTERIOLOGICAL SIGNIFICANCE OF CHRIST'S DESCENT INTO HELL.—Christologically our Lord's Descent into hell must be conceived as an intermediary stage between glorification and abasement. It partook of abasement in respect of the external circumstance of place, but it did not entail upon His human nature any substantial or intrinsic alteration.[26] From the soteriological point of view the question as to the meaning of Christ's Descent into hell resolves itself into another, namely, What was its object or purpose?

What can have been our Saviour's purpose in visiting the patriarchs? We may safely assume that His descent stood in some sort of relation to the redemption of the human race which He had just accomplished. It must have aimed at their beatification, for the limbo contained no reprobates. St. Paul applies the text Ps. LXVII, 19: "*Ascendens in altum captivam duxit captivitatem*" to the inmates of the limbo, — as if he wished to say: Ascending into Heaven Christ leads away with Him those who had been imprisoned in the limbo.[27]

We are informed of the object of our Lord's Descent into the limbo by St. Peter, who says in his

IX, pp. 256 sqq.; Mamachi, *De Animabus Iustorum in Sinu Abrahae ante Christi Mortem*, Rome 1706.

26 Cfr. H. Simar, *Dogmatik*, Vol. I, 3rd ed., p. 538, Freiburg 1899.

27 Cfr. Eph. IV, 8.

first Epistle:[28] "[Christ was] put to death indeed in the flesh, but enlivened in the spirit, in which also coming he preached to those spirits that were in prison:[29] which had been some time incredulous,[30] when they waited for the patience of God in the days of Noe, when the ark was a-building." This text is admittedly difficult of interpretation;[31] but despite a certain obscurity, its general drift is discernable. The Apostle evidently means to say that Christ personally approached[32] the spirits or souls of those who were imprisoned in the limbo and preached[33] to them. What and why did he preach to them? To assume that He tried to convert the damned would contradict the revealed truth that there is no salvation for those condemned to hell. Can it have been His purpose to assure them of their damnation? This hypothesis is equally untenable, because a little further down in his text St. Peter expressly describes Christ's preaching (*κήρυγμα*) as a "gospel," which means a message of joy. "Νεκροῖς εὐηγγελίσθη," these are his words—"the gospel was preached to the dead."[34] The "gospel" which our Lord preached to the inmates of limbo must have been the glad tidings that their imprisonment was at an end. But whom does St. Peter mean when he speaks of "those spirits . . . which had been some time incredulous, when they waited for the patience of God in the days of Noe"? This is a difficult question to answer. But no matter how we may choose to interpret the subsidiary clause, the main sentence is plain enough. Among the just imprisoned in the limbo there were also (*καὶ*) some who had abused God's

28 1 Pet. III, 18 sqq.

29 *ἐν ᾧ καὶ τοῖς ἐν φυλακῇ πνεύμασιν πορευθεὶς ἐκήρυξεν.*

30 *ἀπειθήσασίν ποτε.*

31 Cfr. St. Augustine, *Ep. ad Evod.*, 164.

32 *πορευθείς.*

33 *ἐκήρυξεν*, *praedicavit.*

34 1 Pet. IV, 6.

patience before the Deluge by remaining incredulous till the flood overtook them.[35] The "gospel" or joyful message which Christ brought to the inmates of limbo cannot have consisted in anything more than the preliminary announcement that they were soon to be freed; for their formal admission into the heavenly abode of the Blessed did not take place till the day of His Ascension.[36] Nevertheless, in view of our Lord's remark to the penitent thief: "This day thou shalt be with me in paradise," we must hold that the patriarchs were forthwith admitted to the beatific vision of God.[37]

ARTICLE 3

THE RESURRECTION

1. The Relation of Christ's Resurrection to His Death.—Christ's glorious Resurrection may be considered from three distinct points of view.

Apologetically, *i. e.*, regarded as a historic fact establishing His Divinity, it is the bulwark of our faith [1] and the pledge of our own future resurrection.[2]

Christologically, the Resurrection signalizes

35 Cfr. Hundhausen, *Das erste Pastoralschreiben des Apostelfürsten Petrus*, pp. 343 sqq., Mainz 1873.

36 Cfr. Ps. LXVII, 19.

37 Cfr. the Catechism of the Council of Trent, Part I, Ch. 6, Qu. 6. The reasons why it was meet that Christ should descend into hell are developed by St. Thomas, *S. Theol.*, 3a, qu. 52, art. 1.

1 1 Cor. XV, 14.

2 1 Cor. XV, 13.—For an apologetic treatment of the Resurrection we refer the student to Devivier-Sasia, *Christian Apologetics*, Vol. I, pp. 197 sqq., San Jose, Cal., 1903; G. W. B. Marsh, *The Resurrection of Christ, Is it a Fact?* London 1905; and other similar treatises.

Christ's entrance into the state of glory which He had earned for Himself by His passion and death.[3]

Considered from the distinctive viewpoint of Soteriology, the Resurrection of Christ was not, strictly speaking, the chief, nor even a contributing cause of our redemption;[4] but it was an essential complement thereof, and constituted its triumphant consummation.

a) The Catholic Church regards the Resurrection as an integral, though not an essential, element of the atonement. That is why she mourns on Good Friday and celebrates Easter as the great feast of the Redemption. "Lastly," says the Roman Catechism,[5] ". . . the Resurrection of our Lord was necessary, in order to complete the mystery of our salvation and redemption; for by his death Christ liberated us from our sins, and by His Resurrection he restored to us the principal blessings which we had forfeited by sin. Hence it is said by the Apostle: 'He was delivered up for our sins, and rose again for our justification.'[6] That nothing, therefore, might be wanting to the salvation of the human race, it was meet that, as He should die, He should also rise again." This teaching is in perfect accord with Sacred Scripture, which links the crucifixion of our Lord with His Resurrection and represents both events as one indivisible whole. Cfr. Luke XXIV, 46 sq.: "Thus it is written, and thus it behooved Christ to suffer, and to rise

3 Cfr. Luke XXIV, 26. V. *supra*, pp. 58 sq.

4 The sole cause of our redemption was the Saviour's death on the Cross. (Cfr. *supra*, pp. 85 sqq.)

5 Part I, Ch. 6, Qu. 12.

6 Rom. IV, 25.

again from the dead, the third day, that penance and remission of sins should be preached in his name unto all nations." [7]

b) St. Paul deepened this conception by pointing out that the Crucifixion and the Resurrection contain the two essential elements of justification — remission of sin and infusion of a new life. As Christ died and rose again from the dead, so shall we die to sin and arise to spiritual life. Cfr. Rom. VI, 6 sqq.: "Knowing this, that our old man is crucified with him, that the body of sin may be destroyed, to the end that we may serve sin no longer. For he that is dead is justified from sin. Now if we be dead with Christ, we believe that we shall live also together with Christ: knowing that Christ rising again from the dead, dieth now no more." The Apostle loved to apply this sublime symbolism to the Sacrament of Baptism, in which the acts of immersion and emersion emblem both the burial and Resurrection of Christ, and the liberation from sin and sanctification of the sinner. Cfr. Rom. VI, 4: "For we are buried together with him by baptism into death; that as Christ is risen from the dead by the glory of the Father, so we also may walk in newness of life." [8]

2. THE RESURRECTION OF CHRIST AS A DOGMA. —The glorious Resurrection of our Lord is a cardinal dogma, nay the very foundation and keystone of Christian belief. For this reason the

[7] Cfr. St. Bonaventure, *Comment. in Quatuor Libros Sent.*, III, dist. 19, art. 1, qu. 1: *"Ratio merendi iustificationem attribuitur soli passioni, non resurrectioni; ratio vero terminandi et quietandi attribuitur resurrectioni, ad quam ordinatur iustificatio, non passioni."*

[8] Cfr. 2 Cor. V, 15. On the subject-matter of this subdivision the student may profitably consult St. Thomas, *S. Theol.*, 3a, qu. 56, art. 2 and H. Simar, *Die Theologie des hl. Paulus,* 2nd ed., pp. 194 sqq., Freiburg 1883.

phrase "on the third day He arose again" was embodied in all the creeds and reiterated in numerous doctrinal definitions.

The Catholic Church has always emphasized two distinct points in regard to the Resurrection, *viz.:* (1) Its reality or truth, and (2) the transfigured and glorified state of the risen Redeemer. To safeguard these two aspects of the dogma she strenuously insisted on the real reunion of Christ's soul with His body,[9] and formally rejected the Origenist teaching of the ethereal nature and sphericity of the risen body as well as the heresy of its alleged corruptibility. Thus the Council of Constantinople (A. D. 543) says: "If any one assert that the body of our Lord after the Resurrection was ethereal and spherical in shape, . . . let him be anathema." [10] And the symbol of Pope Leo IX declares that Christ arose from the dead on the third day "by a true resurrection of the flesh, to confirm which He ate with His disciples—not because He stood in need of food, but solely by His will and power." [11] All these statements can be convincingly demonstrated from Divine Revelation.

a) Christ had positively predicted that He would arise on the third day (cfr. Matth. XII, 40;

9 *Cfr. Conc. Lateran. IV, Caput "Firmiter"* (*supra*, p. 91).

10 *"Si quis dixerit Domini corpus post resurrectionem fuisse aethereum et figurâ sphaericâ, anathema sit."* Denzinger's *Fnchiridion*, 9th ed., n. 196.

11 Denzinger-Bannwart, n. 344.

XX, 19; XXVII, 63; Mark X, 34; Luke XVIII, 33; John II, 18 sqq.). He proved the reality and the truth of His resurrection by repeatedly appearing to His disciples, conversing with them, allowing them to touch His sacred body, eating and drinking with them, and so forth. (Matth. XXVIII, 17 sq.; Luke XXIV, 41 sqq.; John XX, 24 sqq.; 1 Cor. XV, 6). The Apostles would not have so courageously and uncompromisingly stood up for their faith in the Resurrection had they not seen and conversed with the risen Lord. Cfr. Acts IV, 33: "And with great power [12] did the Apostles give testimony of the Resurrection of Jesus Christ our Lord." [13] Though not an eye-witness, St. Paul was a bold and enthusiastic herald of the Resurrection: "If Christ be not risen again, then is our preaching vain, and your faith is also vain." [14]

That Christ rose in a glorified body is evidenced by the circumstances surrounding His Resurrection,[15] and by the fact that His risen body was endowed with certain attributes which man cannot enjoy except in a transfigured state.[16]

12 δυνάμει μεγάλῃ, *virtute magnâ.*

13 Cfr. Acts II, 22 sqq.; III, 15; X, 40 sqq.; XIII, 30 sqq.

14 1 Cor. XV, 14; cfr. Rom. X, 9.

15 Matth. XXVIII, 1 sqq.; Luke XXIV, 36 sqq.; John XX, 19 sqq.

16 This point will be developed in Eschatology.

He retained the marks of His five wounds [17] for reasons of congruity, which St. Thomas explains as follows: "It was becoming that the soul of Christ in the Resurrection should reassume the body with its wounds. First, for the glorification of Christ Himself; secondly, to confirm His disciples in their faith in the Resurrection; third, that in supplicating the Father for us, He might always remind Him of what He had suffered for men; fourth to recall the divine mercy to those whom He had redeemed, by exhibiting to them the marks of His death; and, lastly, that on Judgment day He might show forth the justice of the judgment by which [the wicked] are damned." [18]

That Christ really and truly rose from the dead in a glorified body, is so evident from Sacred Scripture that we need not stop to prove it from Tradition.[19]

b) In connection with the Resurrection of our Lord the Catholic Church has always held two other important truths, *viz.*: (1) That His Resurrection is the prototype of a general "resurrection of the flesh," and (2) that Christ arose by His own power.

Both these truths are clearly taught in the famous Creed drawn up by the Eleventh Council of Toledo (A. D. 675): "And on the third day, raised up by His

17 Cfr. John XX, 27; Apoc. V, 6.

18 *S. Theol.*, 3a, qu. 54, art. 4: *"Conveniens fuit animam Christi in resurrectione corpus cum cicatricibus resumere: primo quidem propter gloriam ipsius Christi . . .; secundo ad confirmandum corda discipulorum circa fidem suae resurrectionis; tertio ut Patri pro nobis supplicans, quale genus mortis pro homine pertulerit, semper ostendat; quarto ut sua morte redemptis, quam misericorditer sint adiuti, propositis eiusdem mortis indiciis insinuet; postremo ut in iudicio [ultimo], quam iuste damnentur, ibidem denuntiet."*

19 On the whole subject cfr. Billuart, *De Myst. Christi*, diss. 12, art. 4 and 6; G. B. Tepe, *Inst. Theol.*, Vol. I, pp. 97 sqq., Paris 1894.

own power, He rose again from the grave; by virtue of this example of our Head we profess that there will be a resurrection of the flesh for all the dead."[20] The phrase "by His own power" (*virtute propriâ*) points to an active rising (*resurgere*), which is more than a miraculous awakening (*resuscitari*).

The dogma is clearly contained in Sacred Scripture. Cfr. John II, 19: "Jesus answered and said to them: Destroy this temple, and in three days I will raise it up."[21] John X, 17 sq.: "Therefore doth the Father love me: because I lay down my life, that I may take it again. No man taketh it away from me: but I lay it down of myself, and I have power to lay it down: and I have power to take it up again."[22]

Christ Himself ascribes this power to His consubstantiality with the Father. John V, 21: "For as the Father raiseth up the dead, and giveth life: so the Son also giveth life to whom he will."[23] Hence, if Holy Scripture elsewhere speaks of our Lord's being raised up by the Father,[24] this is obviously an appropriation, based on the fact that the efficient cause of our Saviour's Resurrection was not His humanity, which had been resolved into its constituent elements by death, but His Divinity, which remained hypostatically united with His soul and body. The Roman Catechism explains this as follows: "There existed a divine energy as well in the body, by which it might be reunited to the soul, as in the soul, by which it might return again to the body, and by which He,

20 "*Tertio quoque die virtute propriâ suâ suscitatus a sepulcro resurrexit; hoc ergo exemplo capitis nostri confitemur veram fieri resurrectionem carnis omnium mortuorum.*" Denzinger-Bannwart, n. 286.

21 ἐγερῶ, *excitabo*.

22 ἐξουσίαν ἔχω πάλιν λαβεῖν αὐτήν.

23 ὁ υἱὸς οὓς θέλει ζωοποιεῖ.

24 Acts II, 24 sqq.; III, 13 sqq.; Rom. VIII, 11; Gal. I, 1.

by His own power, might return to life and rise again from the dead."[25]

READINGS: —* Billuart, *De Incarnatione,* diss. 19–20.— IDEM, *De Mysterio Christi,* diss. 9–12.— St. Thomas, *Summa Theologica,* 3a, qu. 19–22; qu. 24, 26; qu. 46–56.— Bellarmine, *De Christo,* l. IV, c. 6-16; l. V, c. 1-10.— De Lugo, *De Mysterio Incarnationis,* disp. 27 sqq..—* Franzelin, *De Verbo Incarnato,* sect. 4, Rome 1881.— Oswald, *Soteriologie,* 2nd ed., Paderborn 1887.—* Stentrup, S. J., *Soteriologia,* 2 vols., Innsbruck 1889.— G. B. Tepe, *Institutiones Theologicae,* Vol. III, pp. 617 sqq., Paris 1896.— Chr. Pesch, S. J., *Praelectiones Dogmaticae,* Vol. IV, 3d ed., pp. 201 sqq., Freiburg 1909.— L. Janssens, *De Deo-Homine,* II, Freiburg 1912. G. Van Noort, *De Deo Redemptore,* 4th ed., by J. P. Verhaar, Hilversum 1925.—P. Galtier, *De Incarnatione et Redemptione,* Paris 1926.—Hunter, *Outlines of Dogmatic Theology,* Vol. II, pp. 506 sqq., London *s. a.*—Wilhelm-Scannell, *A Manual of Catholic Theology,* Vol. II, pp. 181–195, 2nd ed., London 1901.—A. Ritter, *Christus der Erlöser,* Linz 1903.—* B. Dörholt, *Lehre von der Genugtuung Christi,* Paderborn 1896.—Muth, *Heilstat Christi als stellvertretende Genugtuung,* Ratisbon 1904.—K. Staab, *Die Lehre von der stellvertretenden Genugtuung,* Paderborn 1908.—Pell, *Lehre des hl. Athanasius von der Sünde und Erlösung,* Passau 1888.—Sträter, *Erlösungslehre des hl. Athanasius,* Freiburg 1894.—Weigl, *Heilslehre des hl. Cyrill von Alexandrien,* Mainz 1905.—J. Rivière, *Le Dogme de la Rédemption,* Paris 1905 (English translation, *The Doctrine of the Atonement,* 2 vols., London 1909). (A criticism of this work in Chr. Pesch, S. J., *Das Sühneleiden unseres göttlichen Erlösers,* Freiburg i. B. 1916).—E. Krebs, *Der Logos als Heiland im ersten Jahrhundert,* Freiburg 1910.—E. Hugon, O. P., *Le Mystère de la Rédemption* (a speculative pendant to Rivière's *Le Dogme de la Rédemption,* which is mainly historical), Paris 1911.—H. N. Oxenham, *The Catholic Doctrine of the Atonement: An Historical Inquiry into its Development in the Church,* London 1865 (to be read with caution).—J. Kleutgen, S. J., *Theologie der Vorzeit,* Vol. I, 2nd ed., pp. 336 sqq., Münster 1870 (against Günther).—Friedlieb, *Leben Jesu Christi des Erlösers mit neuen historischen und chronologischen*

25 *Cat. Rom.,* P. I, c. 6, qu. 8: "*Divina vis tum in corpore inerat, qua animae iterum coniungit, tum in anima, qua ad corpus reverti posset, qua et licuit suâ virtute reviviscere atque a mortuis resurgere.*"— Cfr. Chr. Pesch, *Praelect. Dogmat.,* Vol. IV, pp. 280 sqq.

Untersuchungen, Paderborn 1887.—Grimm, *Leben Jesu nach den vier Evangelien,* 7 vols., 2nd ed., Ratisbon 1890 sqq.—Didon, O. P., *Jesus Christ,* English edition, London 1895.—J. E. Belser, *Geschichte des Leidens und Sterbens, der Auferstehung und Himmelfahrt des Herrn,* 2nd ed., Freiburg 1913.—W. Humphrey, S. J., *The One Mediator,* London *s. a.*—A. J. Maas, S. J., *Christ in Type and Prophecy,* Vol. II, pp. 13 sqq., New York 1895.—G. W. B. Marsh, *Messianic Philosophy,* pp. 24 sqq., London 1908.—Freddi-Sullivan, S. J., *Jesus Christ the Word Incarnate,* pp. 191 sqq., St. Louis 1904.—J. Tixeront, *Histoire des Dogmes,* Vol. II, 3rd ed., pp. 148 sqq., 285 sqq., 376 sqq., Paris 1909.—B. J. Otten, S. J., *A Manual of the History of Dogmas,* Vol. II, St. Louis 1918, pp. 196 sqq., 201 sqq.—R. Guardini, *Die Lehre des hl. Bonaventura von der Erlösung,* Düsseldorf 1921.—A. Médebielle, *L'Expiation dans l'Ancien et le Nouveau Testament,* Vol. I, Rome 1924.—Ph. E. Hallett, *The Atonement,* (C. T. S. pamphlet), London 1927.—C. Lattey, S. J. (ed.) *The Atonement,* (Papers from the Summer School of Catholic Studies held in Cambridge, 1928), Cambridge, 1928.

On the idea of a *σωτήρ* in the pagan religions of antiquity see, besides E. Krebs, *Der Logos als Heiland* (*supra cit.*), B. Bartmann, *Dogma und Religionsgeschichte,* Paderborn 1922, pp. 30–56.

See also the references in Pohle-Preuss, *Christology,* pp. 7 sq.

* The asterisk before an author's name indicates that his treatment of the question is especially clear and thorough. As St. Thomas is invariably the best guide, the omission of the asterisk before his name never means that we consider his work in any way inferior to that of other writers. There are vast stretches of theology which he scarcely touched.

PART II

THE THREE OFFICES OF THE REDEEMER

The Redemption, considered as an objective fact, must be subjectively appropriated by each individual human being. Hence three functions or offices on the part of our Divine Redeemer, (1) that of High Priest, (2) that of Prophet or Teacher, and (3) that of King.

CHAPTER I

CHRIST'S PRIESTHOOD

SECTION I

CHRIST'S DEATH A TRUE SACRIFICE

The present Chapter is chiefly concerned with demonstrating, (1) that the death of Christ was a true sacrifice, and (2) that He Himself was a true priest. It is these facts which give to the Redemption its sacerdotal and hieratic stamp and furnish us with the key to the philosophy of the atonement.

1. Definition of the Term "Bloody Sacrifice."—A sacrifice is "the external offering up of a visible gift, which is destroyed, or at least submitted to an appropriate transformation, by a lawful minister in recognition of the sovereignty of God and in order to appease His anger."

a) This definition, which will be more fully explained in the dogmatic treatise on the Holy Eucharist, embraces four essential elements:

(*a*) A visible gift and its physical or moral destruction or transformation, such as the slaughtering of an animal, the burning of cereals, the pouring out of a fluid, etc.

(β) A lawful minister or priest who offers the gift to God.

(γ) An exterior act of worship, consisting in the physical presentation of the gift.

(δ) A final end or object, which is the acknowledgment of God's supreme dominion and the appeasement of His anger.

Applying the Scholastic distinction between *materia* and *forma,* we find that the *materia remota* of a sacrifice is the visible gift itself, its *materia proxima,* the act of destruction or transformation, and its *forma,* the sacrificial act (*actio sacrifica*), which combines and unifies both the external offering of the visible gift and the intrinsic purpose for which it is offered. This intrinsic purpose or object is the main factor, because it informs and determines the external act, just as the human soul informs and determines the body. Without a genuine intention on the part of the sacrificing priest there is no sacrifice.[1]

b) The twofold purpose of every sacrifice is the acknowledgment of God's supreme dominion and the appeasement of His anger.

The first of these objects is attained by adoration, the second by expiation.

Adoration is the formal element of every sacrifice, *i. e.,* that which essentially constitutes it a sacrifice in the strict sense of the term. Expiation does not enter into the essence of sacrifice, but is a merely secondary factor, because conditioned by the accidental fact of sin. Since both thanksgiving and supplication, when addressed to the Almighty, invariably and necessarily partake of the

[1] Cfr. St. Thomas, *S. Theol.,* 2a 2ae, qu. 85, art 2.

nature of absolute worship, sacrifices offered up for these two purposes have no relation to sin. The case is different with expiatory sacrifices. While sin has neither abolished nor debased, but rather reinforced, the main purpose of adoration, namely thanksgiving and supplication, it has added a new object which, though in itself secondary, has become inseparable from the notion of sacrifice in consequence of the Fall.

These considerations explain the usual division into sacrifices of adoration (*sacrificia latreutica*), sacrifices of thanksgiving (*sacrificia eucharistica*), sacrifices of supplication or petition (*sacrificia impetratoria*), and sacrifices of expiation or propitiation (*sacrificia propitiatoria*). As these four objects can never be entirely separated, the various kinds of sacrifice owe their specific appellations solely to the special emphasis laid on the principal purpose for which each is offered.

c) A most important element in the concept of sacrifice is the symbolic substitution of some other creature for man. "The gift takes the place of the giver. By sacrificing an object over which he has control, and offering it up entirely to God, man acknowledges God's overlordship over his person and life, and it is the latter which is symbolically offered up and destroyed."[2] This symbolism is based on the very nature of sacrifice. The acknowledgment of God as the sovereign Lord of the universe has its human correlative in man's humble subjection and surrender of himself to his Maker. The most precious gift which man has received from God is life. Since he cannot surrender this — God demands no human sacrifices — He offers it up symbolically by destroying or transforming and present-

2 Jos. Dahlmann, S. J., *Der Idealismus der indischen Religionsphilosophie im Zeitalter der Opfermystik*, p. 22, Freiburg 1901.

ing in his own stead some living or inanimate creature. This vicarious act assumes its deepest significance in the sacrifice of propitiation, by which, in addition to manifesting the sentiments already mentioned, man confesses his guilt and admits that he has deserved death in punishment for his sins. It is in this sense that St. Thomas explains the Old Testament holocausts. "The slaughtering of animals," he says, "signifies the destruction of sins and that men are deserving of death for their sins, as if those animals were killed in their stead to denote the expiation of their sins."[3] The ethical significance of sacrifice is based on this same consideration. The highest act of divine worship, coupled as it ever should be with sincere contrition and an ardent desire to be reconciled to God, cannot but elevate, cleanse, and sanctify the human heart, especially in view of the fact that God's will to save all men and the legitimate institution of the sacrificial rite confirm human expectation and constitute a rich source of consolation.

d) The Sacrifice of the Cross is not only a true sacrifice, but in contradistinction to the *sacrificium incruentum* (Hebrew, מִנְחָה) specifically a bloody sacrifice. What constitutes the difference between the two? It cannot be the person of the lawful minister, nor yet the final object of all sacrifice (except in so far as propitiation must plainly be the prevailing motive of every bloody sacrifice). Hence we shall have to

[3] *S. Theol.*, 1a 2ae, qu. 102, art. 3, ad 5: "*Per occisionem animalium significatur destructio peccatorum et quod homines erant digni occisione pro peccatis suis, ac si illa animalia loco eorum occiderentur ad significandam expiationem peccatorum.*" Cfr. N. Giehr, *The Holy Sacrifice of the Mass*, pp. 35 sqq., 3rd ed., St. Louis 1908.

seek for the specific difference in the *materia* and *forma*.

The *materia remota* of a bloody sacrifice, as its very name suggests, must be a living creature endowed with blood (*victima, hostia*). Its *materia proxima* is the slaying of the victim, accompanied by an effusion of the life-giving fluid (*mactatio cum sanguinis effusione*). In regard to the physical *forma* there is room for a difference of opinion, as we do not know for certain whether the sacrificial act (*actio sacrifica*), strictly so called, is the slaying of the victim or its oblation. The latter opinion is the more probable, though not certain. First, because the act of slaying, as such, with its consequent shedding of blood, does not necessarily indicate the purpose of the sacrifice, and consequently requires a more specific determinant, *i. e.*, the act of oblation. Secondly, because in the Mosaic sacrifice the victim was slain by laymen and temple servants, while the oblation of the blood was a function reserved to the lawfully appointed priesthood.[4] Third, because it is impossible to assume that Christ's bloody sacrifice on the Cross consisted in the material acts of cruelty committed by His barbarous executioners.

Hence a bloody sacrifice must be defined as "the visible oblation of a living creature, the slaying of which is accompanied by the shedding of blood, by a lawful minister, in acknowledgment of the supreme sovereignty of God, and especially to propitiate His anger."[5]

2. THE DOGMA.—The Church has formally defined, against the Socinians and the Rationalists,

4 Cfr. P. Scholz, *Die hl. Altertümer des Volkes Israel*, II, 134 sqq., Ratisbon 1868.

5 Cfr. Becanus, *De Triplici Sacrificio, Naturae, Legis, Gratiae*, Opusc. II, Lugduni 1631.

that Christ's vicarious atonement was a bloody sacrifice, made for the purpose of reconciling the human race to God (*sacrificium propitiatorium.*)

The Council of Ephesus (A. D. 431) declared against Nestorius: "For He offered Himself up for us as an odor of sweetness to God the Father. Hence if any one say that the Divine Logos Himself was not made our High Priest [6] and Apostle . . . let him be anathema." [7] The Council of Trent, in defining the Holy Sacrifice of the Mass, bases its definition on the dogma that Christ's bloody death on the Cross was a true sacrifice: "Though He was about to offer Himself once on the altar of the Cross unto God the Father . . . that He might leave a visible sacrifice . . . whereby that bloody sacrifice, once to be accomplished on the Cross, might be represented, . . . He offered up to God the Father His own body and blood under the species of bread and wine . . . [In the Mass] that same Christ is contained and immolated in an unbloody manner, who once offered Himself in a bloody manner on the altar of the Cross. . . . For the victim is one and the same, the same now offering by the ministry of priests, who then offered Himself on the Cross, the manner alone of offering being different." [8]

6 ἀρχιερέα.

7 "*Obtulit enim semetipsum pro nobis in odorem suavitatis Deo et Patri. Si quis ergo Pontificem et Apostolum nostrum dicit factum non ipsum Dei Verbum . . ., anathema sit.*" *Synod. Ephes.*, can. 10. (Denzinger-Bannwart, n. 122.)

8 "*Etsi semel seipsum in ara crucis morte intercedente Deo Patri oblaturus erat, . . . ut relinqueret sacrificium, quo cruentum illud semel in cruce peragendum repraesentaretur, . . . corpus et sanguinem suum sub speciebus panis et vini Deo Patri obtulit. . . . [In Missa] idem ille Christus . . . incruente immolatur, qui in ara crucis semel seipsum cruente obtulit . . . Una eademque est hostia, idem nunc offerens sacerdotum ministerio, qui seipsum tunc in cruce obtulit, solâ*

a) The Scriptural proof of our dogma is based partly on the Old and partly on the New Testament.

α) The argument from the Old Testament may be stated in the terms of a syllogism, thus: The sacrifices of the Old Law, which were almost exclusively bloody oblations, culminated in the idea that the Israelite, conscious of having deserved death for his sins, substituted brute animals in his own stead and offered them to God as a means of propitiation. Now all the sacrifices of the Old Law were merely types of Christ's death on the Cross. Therefore Christ's death must be as truly a vicarious sacrifice of blood and propitiation as were the sacrifices of the Old Testament.

Proof of the Major Premise. There is no need of demonstrating the proposition that the Old Testament sacrifices were true sacrifices, as this is denied by no one. That the Jews practiced symbolic substitution is obvious from the sacrificial rites which they employed. Aside from certain unbloody oblations of altogether minor importance they offered three different kinds of sacrifices: burnt offerings, peace offerings, and offerings for sin. All three required the imposition of hands on the head of the victim to symbolize that the sins of the people were heaped upon it. Thus, when the multitude had transgressed a divine command through ignorance, they had to bring a sin-offering to the door of the taber-

offerendi ratione diversâ." (*Conc. Trid.*, Sess. XXII, cap. 1 and 2 Denzinger Bannwart, No. 938 and 940; cfr. also can. 3–4, *ibid.* n. 950, 951.)

nacle in the shape of a calf. Lev. IV, 13–20: "And the ancients of the people shall put their hands upon the head thereof before the Lord; and the calf being immolated in the sight of the Lord, the priest that is anointed shall carry off the blood into the tabernacle of the testimony. . . . And the priest praying for them, the Lord will be merciful unto them." On the Feast of Expiation two buck goats were led up to the door of the tabernacle, and one of them was slain as a sin offering. With regard to the other the Mosaic law ordained as follows: "Then let him [the high priest] offer the living goat: and putting both hands upon his head, let him confess all the iniquities of the children of Israel, and all their offences and sins: and praying that they may light on his head, he shall turn him out by a man ready for it, into the desert. And when the goat hath carried all their iniquities into an uninhabited land, and shall be let go into the desert, Aaron shall return into the tabernacle of the testimony." [9] What was thus symbolized in the sacrificial rite is explicitly set forth in the prohibition of blood, Lev. XVII, 11: ". . . the life of the flesh is in the blood: and I have given it to you, that you may make atonement with it upon the altar for your souls, and the blood may be for an expiation of the soul." The text we have previously quoted from Isaias (Is. LIII, 4 sqq.), derives its deeper significance from the sacrificial rite described by the same prophet (Is. LII, 15; LIII, 7, 10).[10]

Proof of the Minor Premise. The minor premise of our syllogism can be demonstrated from St. Paul's Epistle to the Hebrews, particularly Chapters 8 to 10. As the Old Law had but "a shadow of the good things to

9 Lev. XVI, 9; XVI, 20 sqq.

10 *Supra*, p. 46. Cfr. Knabenbauer, *Erklärung des Propheten Isaias*, Freiburg 1881.

come,"[11] so in particular its sacrifices merely prefigured the one great sin-offering on the Cross. Being "weak and needy elements," it was impossible that "the blood of oxen and goats" should "take away sin."[12] The student will be able to appreciate the full force of this argument only after a careful perusal of the whole Epistle. If the Mosaic sacrifices were real and vicarious, this must be true in a far higher sense of the sacrifice of the Cross, which they foreshadowed.[13]

β) The argument from the New Testament is based on the Epistle to the Hebrews, with its explicit assertion that the typical sacrifices of the Old Law found their consummation and perfection in the one true sacrifice of the Cross. In a variety of phrases St. Paul reiterates the fundamental truth that, as priest and victim in one person, Jesus Christ by a single bloody offering atoned for the sins of men and once for all consummated their eternal salvation.

To quote only a few salient passages: "For if the blood of goats and of oxen, and the ashes of an heifer being sprinkled, sanctify such as are defiled, to the cleansing of the flesh: how much more shall the blood of Christ, who by the Holy Ghost offered himself unspotted unto God,[14] cleanse our conscience from dead works to serve the living God?"[15] "So also Christ was offered once to exhaust the sins of many."[16] "In

11 Heb. X, 1.

12 Heb. X, 4. Cfr. Gal. IV, 9.

13 Cfr. Franzelin, *De Verbo Incarnato*, thes. 49, Rome 1881; Hugo Weiss, *Die messianischen Vorbilder im Alten Testament*, Freiburg 1905.

14 ἑαυτὸν προσήνεγκεν ἄμωμον τῷ Θεῷ.

15 Heb. IX, 13–14.

16 ἅπαξ προσενεχθεὶς εἰς τὸ πολλῶν ἀνενεγκεῖν ἁμαρτίας. Heb. IX, 28.

the which will we are sanctified by the oblation of the body of Jesus Christ alone."[17] "But this man [Christ] offering one sacrifice for sins,[18] for ever sitteth on the right hand of God."[19] "For by one oblation[20] he hath perfected for ever them that are sanctified."[21]

The sacrificial character of the death of our Divine Lord is expressly inculcated in many other passages of the New Testament.

Cfr. Matth. XX, 28: "*Filius hominis non venit ministrari, sed ministrare et dare animam suam redemptionem pro multis*[22]— The Son of man is not come to be ministered unto, but to minister, and to give his life a redemption for many." Christ here emphasizes three momenta, *viz.:* sacrifice, atonement, and the vicarious character of that atonement. "To give one's life"[23] is a distinctly hieratic and sacrificial term; "for many"[24] denotes vicarious satisfaction, and "redemption"[25] indicates expiation. It follows from this important text that the expression "for many" or "for all,"[26] which occurs so frequently in the New Testament, when used in connection with sacrifice means, not only "for the benefit of many," but also "instead of many." Cfr. Eph. V, 2: "*Tradidit semetipsum pro nobis oblationem et hostiam Deo*[27] *in odorem suavitatis* — Christ . . . hath delivered himself for us, an oblation and a sacrifice to God for an odor of sweetness."[28] I Tim. II, 6:

17 Heb. X, 10.

18 μιὰν ὑπὲρ ἁμαρτιῶν προσενέγκας θυσίαν.

19 Heb. X, 12.

20 μιᾷ γὰρ προσφορᾷ.

21 Heb. X, 14.

22 καὶ δοῦναι τὴν ψυχὴν αὐτοῦ λύτρον ἀντὶ πολλῶν.

23 δοῦναι τὴν ψυχήν.

24 ἀντὶ πολλῶν, not merely ὑπὲρ πολλῶν.

25 λύτρον (strictly, *ransom*).

26 ὑπὲρ πολλῶν, *pro multis*.

27 παρέδωκεν ἑαυτὸν ὑπὲρ ἡμῶν προσφορὰν καὶ θυσίαν.

28 προσφορά here means sacrifice in general, θυσία, bloody sacrifice.

"*Qui dedit redemptionem semetipsum pro omnibus,*[29] *testimonium temporibus suis* — Who gave himself a redemption for all, a testimony in due times." Referring to the Old Testament sacrifice of the Paschal lamb, St. Paul says in his first Epistle to the Corinthians (V, 7): "*Pascha nostrum immolatus est Christus* — For Christ our pasch is sacrificed." The expiatory character of our Lord's death is expressly asserted in Rom. III, 25: "*Quem proposuit Deus propitiationem*[30] *per fidem in sanguine ipsius* — Whom God hath proposed to be a propitiation, through faith in his blood," and likewise in the first Epistle of St. John (II, 2): "*Ipse est propitiatio*[31] *pro peccatis nostris, non pro nostris autem tantum, sed etiam pro totius mundi* — He is the propitiation for our sins: and not for ours only, but also for those of the whole world."[32]

b) Christian Tradition has from the first faithfully adhered to the obvious teaching of Holy Scripture in this matter.

The so-called Epistle of Barnabas, which was probably composed at the time of the Emperor Nerva (A. D. 96–98),[33] contains the following passage: "For our sins he was going to offer the vessel of the spirit [*i. e.*, His sacred humanity] as a sacrifice,[34] in order that the type established in Isaac, who was sacrificed upon the altar, might be fulfilled."[35] Tertullian expresses himself in a similar strain: "Christ, who was led like a sheep to

29 Ἀντίλυτρον here means a ransom given vicariously, by a representative.

30 ἱλαστήριον = a sacrifice of propitiation.—Cfr. *St. Paul's Concept of* Ἱλαστήριον, by R. A. Mollaun, O. F. M., Washington, D. C., 1923.

31 ἱλασμός.

32 Cfr. 2 Cor. V, 21.

33 Cfr. Bardenhewer-Shahan, *Patrology*, p. 24.

34 ἔμελλε . . . προσφέρειν θυσίαν.

35 *Ep. Barn.*, c. 7, n. 3. (Ed. Funk, I, 23.)

the slaughtering pen, had to be made a sacrifice for all nations." [36]

3. Theological Problems.—Christ vicariously made atonement for us by immolating Himself; consequently, He is priest, acceptant, and victim all in one. This gives rise to a number of subtle theological problems, which in the main may be reduced to three: (a) Was it in His Godhead or manhood that Christ combined the double function of victim and priest? (b) In what sense did He simultaneously offer and accept the sacrifice of the Cross? (c) Wherein precisely did the *actio sacrifica* of His bloody sacrifice consist?

a) The first question must be decided on Christological principles as follows. The victim (*victima, hostia*) of the sacrifice of the Cross was the Godman, or, more specifically, the Divine Logos in person, though not, of course, through the functions of His Divine, but those of His human nature.

To assert that the human nature of our Lord alone was sacrificed on the Cross would be equivalent to Nestorianism. To hold that it was the Godhead as such that was crucified and sacrificed, would savor of Theopaschitic Monophysitism. Both heretical extremes are avoided by saying that the Divine Logos was indeed

36 *Adv. Iud.*, c. 13. For other Patristic texts bearing on this subject see Dörholt, *Die Lehre von der Genugtuung Christi*, § 7-10, Paderborn 1891.

sacrificed (*principium quod*), but only according to His passible manhood (*principium quo*). This proposition is an immediate deduction from the dogma of the Hypostatic Union.

A similar answer may be given to the cognate question: In what way did Christ officiate as a priest? In other words, Did He offer the sacrifice of the Cross (*i. e.*, Himself) to God in His human or in His Divine Nature? The correct answer depends on a true conception of the nature of the Hypostatic Union. Nestorius believed that Jesus Christ and the Logos-Son were two separate and distinct persons, and hence he was entirely consistent in teaching that the man Jesus alone was a high priest, to the exclusion of the Divine Logos.[37] The same conclusion was forced upon the Socinians, who denied the Trinity and consequently also the Divinity of Jesus Christ. Though the Monophysites held a diametrically opposite opinion, they too were perfectly consistent in regarding the Divine Nature of Christ as the instrument of mediation, redemption, and the priesthood; for they imagined Christ's humanity to have been absorbed and destroyed by His Divinity. We cannot, however, regard without surprise the illogical attitude of certain older Protestant divines, who, despite their orthodox teaching on the Hypostatic Union, either showed Nestorian leanings, as *e. g.* Francis Stancarus (d. 1574), or, like certain Calvinists and Zwinglians in Switzerland, adopted the Monophysitic view that Christ was our Mediator and High Priest *qua* Logos and not *qua* man.[38] The truth lies between these extremes. The Godman was a true priest, not, however, in His divine, but solely in His human nature.[39]

37 Cfr. *Concilium Ephes.*, can. 10. V. *supra*, p. 116.

38 For details consult Bellarmine, *De Christo*, V, 2–3.

39 Cfr. St. Thomas, *S. Theol.*, 3a, qu. 22, art. 2.

b) The second question is: How are we to conceive the relation of Christ in His capacity as sacrificing priest, to Christ as the Divine Logos, to whom the sacrifice of the Cross was offered? To solve this problem correctly we shall have to bear in mind the truths set forth in the first part of this treatise with regard to the mediatorship of our Lord.[40]

It will not do to represent the first Person of the Blessed Trinity as the sole acceptor of the sacrifice of the Cross, and Christ merely as the sacrificing priest, though this opinion has found some defenders among Catholic divines. It was the Trinity, or God *qua* God, who had been offended by sin; consequently the sacrifice of the Cross had to be offered up as a propitiation to the entire Trinity. Hence Christ not only offered up the sacrifice of the Cross, but He also accepted it, though of course only in His capacity as God, conjointly with the Father and the Holy Ghost. The Patristic phrase, adopted by the Council of Trent, that Christ "offered Himself unto God the Father," must therefore be explained as an appropriation.[41]

From what we have said it appears that Christ exercised in a most wonderful manner three distinct functions, *viz.:* that of sacrificial victim, that of the sacrificing priest, and that of the accepting God. As God He accepts His own sacrifice; as Godman (or Logos) He is both victim (*victima*) and sacrificing priest (*sacerdos*), though only according to His human nature. St. Augustine

40 *Supra,* pp. 5 sqq.

41 V. *supra,* pp. 67 sq. On the Divine Appropriations see Pohle-Preuss, *The Divine Trinity,* pp. 244 sqq.

beautifully explains this in his famous work *De Civitate Dei.* "And hence that true Mediator, in so far as, by assuming the form of a servant, He became the Mediator between God and men, the man Christ Jesus, though in the form of God He received [accepted] sacrifice together with the Father, with whom He is one God, yet in the form of a servant He chose rather to be than to receive a sacrifice, that not even by this instance any one might have occasion to suppose that sacrifice should be rendered to any creature. Thus He is both the Priest who offers and the Sacrifice offered." [42]

c) As regards the sacrificial act itself, it did not formally consist in the killing of the victim.

To hold that it did, would involve the blasphemous conclusion that the sacrificing priests on Calvary were the brutal soldiers who tortured our Lord and nailed Him to the Cross. No, the real priest was Jesus Christ Himself; His executioners were merely unconscious instruments in the hands of Providence.

If Christ was the sacrificing priest, it follows that He alone performed the sacrificial act.

This sacrificial act did not consist in self-immolation. That would have been sheer suicide. It consisted in the voluntary oblation of His Blood, which He allowed to be shed (extrinsic factor) and which He offered to Almighty God with a true sacrificial intent (intrinsic factor). It was this voluntary oblation of His life and blood

42 *De Civ. Dei*, X, 20. "*Verus ille mediator, inquantum formam servi accipiens mediator effectus est Dei et hominum, homo Christus Iesus, quum in forma Dei sacrificium cum Patre sumat* [*acceptet*], *cum quo et unus Deus est, tamen in forma servi sacrificium maluit esse quam sumere, ne vel hac occasione quisquam existimaret cuilibet sacrificandum esse creaturae. Per hoc et sacerdos est, ipse offerens, ipse et oblatio.*" (Cfr. *De Trinit.*, IV, 14, 19).

(*oblatio vitae et sanguinis*) which constituted the formal element, and consequently the essence of the sacrifice of the Cross.[43]

This also explains why martyrdom is not a true sacrifice. It has not been instituted as such by God, and, furthermore, no martyr can dispose of his life and blood with the sovereign liberty enjoyed by our Lord, who had absolute control over all the circumstances surrounding His death and gave up His soul when and how He pleased.[44]

43 Cfr. John X, 18.

44 Cfr. Franzelin, *De Verbo Incarnato*, thes. 50; Belser, *Das Evangelium des hl. Johannes*, pp. 511 sqq., Freiburg 1905.

SECTION 2

CHRIST A TRUE PRIEST

"Priest" and "Sacrifice" being correlative terms, the priesthood of our Lord Jesus Christ is a logical and necessary corollary of His sacrifice on the Cross. Sacred Scripture expressly confirms this deduction.

The concept of "priesthood" embraces two essential elements, *viz.:* (1) unction or ordination, and (2) the offering of sacrifice. To these may be added, as an integral part, sacerdotal prayer. In the case of Christ, moreover, the Bible lays special stress (3) on the eternity of His priesthood. We shall develop these considerations in the form of three separate theses.

Thesis I: Christ's unction or ordination to the office of high priest took place at the moment of His Incarnation.

This thesis voices the common teaching of Catholic divines.

Proof. If, as we shall show in our next thesis, Christ was truly "a priest according to the order of Melchisedech,"[1] His priesthood must have begun simultaneously with His Incarnation, *i. e.*, at the moment in which the Divine Logos assumed human flesh in the womb of the Virgin. The Divine Logos could not have been a priest be-

1 Heb. V, 6; VI, 20.

fore His Incarnation, because then He was not yet the Godman. Nor was He anointed or consecrated by any special act subsequent to His Incarnation. Hence His ordination must have coincided with the inception of the Hypostatic Union.

This view is confirmed by St. Paul in his Epistle to the Hebrews. Heb. X, 5: "*Ideo ingrediens mundum*[2] *dicit: Hostiam et oblationem noluisti, corpus autem aptasti mihi* — Wherefore when he cometh into the world, he saith: Sacrifice and oblation thou wouldest not: but a body thou hast fitted to me."[3] Here the "fitting of a body" for the sacrifice of the Cross, and consequently the beginning of Christ's priesthood, is represented as coincident with His "coming into the world," *i. e.,* His conception.

In the fifth chapter of the same Epistle the Apostle emphasizes the fact that "every high priest taken from among men, is ordained for men in the things that appertain to God," and then declares that Christ did not ordain Himself, but was "called by God." Heb. V, 4 sq.: "*Nec quisquam sumit sibi honorem, sed qui vocatur a Deo*[4] *tamquam Aaron; sic et Christus non semetipsum clarificavit, ut pontifex fieret,*[5] *sed qui locutus est ad eum* [=*Pater*]: *Filius meus es tu, ego hodie genui te* — Neither doth any man take the honor to himself, but he that is called by God, as Aaron was. So Christ also did not glorify himself, that he might be made a high priest; but he that said unto him: Thou art my Son, this day have I begotten thee."[6] The "call" to the priesthood which Christ received from His Father was

2 εἰσερχόμενος εἰς τόν κόσμον.

3 Cfr. Ps. XXXIX, 7.

4 καλούμενος ἀπὸ τοῦ Θεοῦ.

5 γενηθῆναι ἀρχιερέα.

6 Heb. V, 4 sq.

the command to redeem the human race. This command went into effect at the moment of His conception. Consequently, Christ's priesthood began simultaneously with the *unio hypostatica*.

A third argument for our thesis is based on the Saviour's proper name, *Christus,* which means the Anointed One κατ' ἐξοχήν.[7] Whereas the Levites of the Old Testament were anointed to the ministry by an accidental unction with visible oil,[8] the Godman Jesus Christ, by virtue of the Hypostatic Union, is substantially anointed with the invisible oil of Divinity. This substantial unction, on account of the object and purpose of the Redemption, stands in intimate relationship to the priestly function which He exercised in offering the sacrifice of the Cross, and therefore the Hypostatic Union as such must be regarded as Christ's substantial ordination to the priesthood.

Some of the Fathers appear to teach that our Lord's ordination took place before His Incarnation. It is to be noted, however, that their manner of expression is distinctly proleptic. What they mean is, that it was by His Incarnation that the not yet incarnate Logos was constituted a priest. Certain other Fathers seem to regard Christ's baptism in the Jordan as the beginning of His priesthood. Rightly understood, however, these Fathers do not assert that Christ became a high priest when He received baptism, but merely that he exercised His priesthood for the first time on that occasion. There is a clear-cut distinction between an office and the exercise of its functions; the former differs from the latter as potency differs from act.[9]

7 Cfr. Pohle-Preuss, *Christology,* pp. 228 sq.

8 Cfr. Exod. XXIX, 1 sqq.; Lev. VIII, 1 sqq.

9 Cfr. Petavius, *De Incarn.,* XII, 3 and 11.

Thesis II: During His terrestrial life Christ was a true high priest who exercised His sacerdotal functions by offering sacrifice and prayer.

This proposition embodies an article of faith.

Proof. The Council of Trent defines: *"Quoniam sub priori Testamento teste Apostolo Paulo propter levitici sacerdotii imbecillitatem consummatio non erat, oportuit Deo Patre misericordiarum ita ordinante sacerdotem alium secundum ordinem Melchisedech surgere D. N. Iesum Christum, qui posset omnes, quotquot sanctificandi essent, consummare et ad perfectum adducere."* Anglice: "Forasmuch as, under the former Testament, according to the testimony of the Apostle Paul, there was no perfection, because of the weakness of the Levitical priesthood; there was need, God the Father of mercies so ordaining, that another priest should rise, according to the order of Melchisedech, our Lord Jesus Christ, who might consummate, and lead to what is perfect, as many as were to be sanctified." [10]

The heretical antithesis of this dogma is the Socinian teaching that the priesthood of our Lord was in no sense an earthly but exclusively a heavenly priesthood.[11]

a) That the priesthood of our Divine Lord

10 *Conc. Trid.*, Sess. XXII, cap. 1. (Denzinger-Bannwart, n. 938.)

11 Cfr. F. Socinus, *De Christo Servatore*, P. II, c. 15.

was really and truly an earthly priesthood can easily be proved from Sacred Scripture.

α) To begin with the Old Testament, we need but point to Psalm CIX, the Messianic character of which is guaranteed by Christ Himself.[12] The fourth verse reads as follows: "Thou art a priest for ever according to the order of Melchisedech." Melchisedech was an earthly priest; consequently the priesthood of Christ must be an earthly priesthood.[13]

β) The prophet Isaias, pointing to the "Man of sorrows," *i. e.*, the future Messias, presages that "he shall sprinkle many nations."[14] This sprinkling, from the context, can only mean a sacrificial sprinkling with blood (*aspersio sanguinis*).[15]

γ) No other sacred writer has portrayed the earthly priesthood of our Lord so grandly as St. Paul, whose Epistle to the Hebrews constitutes one prolonged refutation of Socinianism.[16] The gist of this Epistle may be summarized as follows: The priesthood of Melchisedech was far superior to the Levitical priesthood, but the priesthood of Christ is infinitely superior even

12 Matth. XXIII, 43 sqq.

13 On the heresy of the Melchisedechians (who held that Melchisedech was not a man but an incarnation of the Logos) see St. Augustine, *De Haeres.*, n. 34; cfr. Blunt, *Dictionary of Sects,* pp. 304 sq., new impression, London 1903.

14 Is. LII, 15.

15 Cfr. Is. LIII, 3 sqq.; Lev. XVI, 18 sq.; Heb. IX, 14 sqq.

16 A detailed analysis of St. Paul's Epistle to the Hebrews will be found in Franzelin, *De Verbo Incarnato,* thes. 48, n. ii; cfr. also Chr. Pesch, *Prael. Dogmat.,* Vol. IV, 3rd ed., pp. 291 sq.

to the priesthood of Melchisedech. Therefore, Christ is the holiest, the greatest, the most perfect, in fact the sole High Priest, and He exercised His priesthood in the perfect sacrifice of the Cross.[17]

b) But the sacrifice of the Cross was not the only sacerdotal function performed by our Divine Redeemer. He also officiated as High Priest when, at the Last Supper, He instituted the Holy Sacrifice of the Mass, and when He pronounced the sublime prayer for His disciples recorded in the seventeenth chapter of the Gospel of St. John.[18]

A priest does not always pray in his official capacity as priest; some of his prayers are strictly private and personal. It is only when he pronounces portions of the sacrificial rite, such as the Mass, or liturgical prayers intimately connected therewith, as those of the Breviary, that his prayer assumes a sacerdotal or hieratic character. Christ's prayer for His disciples was a strictly sacerdotal or hieratic act, because of its intimate relation to the sacrifice of the Cross. The same is true of the prayers which He uttered at the crucifixion. It is rather difficult to draw a clear-cut line of demarcation between strictly hieratic and purely private prayers in the case of our Divine Lord, because His whole interior life was inseparably interwoven with His mission as the Saviour of mankind, and therefore also with His priesthood. However, we may apply the term "private" in a wider sense to those

17 The Patristic argument for our thesis is developed by Pesch, *op. cit.*, pp. 292 sq. The teaching of the Scholastics on Christ's earthly priesthood may be best studied in St. Thomas, *Summa Theologica*, 3a, qu. 22 art. 1.

18 John XVII, 1–26.

prayers which He offered up, not for His Apostles, or the human race in general, but for Himself, in order to obtain personal favors from His Heavenly Father, as, for instance, when He asked on Mount Olivet that the chalice be removed from His lips,[19] or when He petitioned for His own glorification.

There is an essential difference between prayer and sacrifice, which should be emphasized here. Christ was able to pray for Himself, but He was not able to offer sacrifice for Himself. This has been clearly defined by the Council of Ephesus (A. D. 431): "If any one . . . assert that He [Christ] offered Himself as a sacrifice for Himself, and not rather for us alone, (for He who knew absolutely no sin needed no sacrifice), let him be anathema." [20]

Thesis III: Christ's priesthood continues everlastingly in Heaven.

This proposition also embodies an article of faith.

Proof. In Christology [21] we concluded from the eternity of Christ's priesthood to the inseparability of the Hypostatic Union. Here we have to prove the antecedent. The eternity of Christ's priesthood is an article of faith, because clearly contained in Sacred Scripture. But the manner in which He exercises His sacerdotal

19 Cfr. Heb. V, 7.

20 "*Si quis . . . dicit, quod pro se obtulisset semetipsum oblationem, et non potius pro nobis solis (non enim eguit oblatione, qui peccatum omnino nescivit), anathema sit.*" *Conc. Eph.*, can. 10 (Denzinger-Bannwart, n. 122).—On Christ's praying cfr. St. Thomas, *S. Theol.*, 3a, qu. 21 and L. Janssens, *De Deo-Homine*, Vol. I, pp. 720 sqq., Freiburg 1901.

21 Pohle-Preuss, *Christology*, pp. 74 sqq.

office in Heaven remains to be determined by theological reasoning.

a) The eternity of our Lord's priesthood is taught both directly and indirectly in St. Paul's Epistle to the Hebrews.

α) The Apostle expressly applies to Christ the Messianic verse: "Thou art a priest for ever[22] according to the order of Melchisedech."[23] That "for ever" in this passage means eternity, not *a parte ante* but *a parte post,* and in the strict sense of the term, appears from St. Paul's way of arguing in Heb. VII, 1 sqq., where he opposes our Lord's "everlasting priesthood" to the temporal priesthood of the Levites. Moreover, he distinctly says in Heb. VII, 23 sq.: *"Alii quidem plures facti sunt sacerdotes, idcirco quod morte prohiberentur permanere; hic autem eo quod maneat in aeternum,*[24] *sempiternum habet sacerdotium*[25]— And the others indeed were made many priests, because by reason of death they were not suffered to continue: but this, for that he continueth for ever, hath an everlasting priesthood."

β) Regarding the manner in which Christ exercises His eternal priesthood in Heaven, Revelation teaches us nothing beyond the fact that He is "always living to make intercession for us,"[26] which is a truly sacerdotal function, because, as St. Paul assures us, it bears an intimate relation to the sacrifice of the Cross. Hence we may

22 εἰς τὸν αἰῶνα.

23 Ps. CIX, 4.

24 διὰ τὸ μένειν αὐτὸν εἰς τὸν αἰῶνα.

25 ἀπαράβατον ἔχει τὴν ἱερωσύνην.

26 Heb. VII, 25; Rom. VIII, 34.

conclude that our Lord's intercession for us in Heaven consists in everlastingly asserting the sacrifice of the Cross.

Cfr. Heb. VII, 24 sqq.: "*Sempiternum habet sacerdotium; unde et salvare in perpetuum potest accedentes per semetipsum ad Deum, semper vivens ad interpellandum pro nobis: talis enim*[27] *decebat ut nobis esset pontifex,*[28] . . . *qui non habet necessitatem quotidie* . . . *hostias offerre; hoc enim fecit semel seipsum offerendo* —[He] hath an everlasting priesthood, whereby he is able also to save for ever them that come to God by him; always living to make intercession for us. For it was befitting that we should have such a high priest . . . who needeth not daily . . . to offer sacrifices . . . for this he did once, in offering himself."

St. John, too, describes Christ's heavenly intercession as intimately connected with and based upon the sacrifice of the Cross. Cfr. 1 John II, 1 sq.: "*Sed et si quis peccaverit, advocatum*[29] *habemus apud Patrem Iesum Christum iustum; et ipse est propitiatio*[30] *pro peccatis nostris* — But if any man sin, we have an advocate with the Father, Jesus Christ the just: and he is the propitiation for our sins." The same Apostle in the Apocalypse represents Christ figuratively as a slain lamb, *i. e.*, a transfigured sacrificial victim. Apoc. V, 6: "*Et vidi* . . . *Agnum stantem tamquam occisum*[31] — And I saw . . . a Lamb standing as it were slain." In this light St. Ambrose's conception of the relation existing between Christ's heavenly intercession and the marks of the five wounds in His glorified body, as indelible witnesses

27 γάρ.
28 ἀρχιερεύς.
29 παράκλητον.
30 ἱλασμός = a sacrifice of propitiation.
31 ὡς ἐσφαγμένον.

of His bloody sacrifice, must appeal to us as profoundly significant: "He refused to relinquish the wounds which He had received for us, but preferred to take them with Him to Heaven, in order to exhibit [them] to His Heavenly Father [as] the purchase price of our liberty." [32]

b) The doctrine of Christ's eternal priesthood in Heaven has given rise to three separate theological problems: (α) What is the precise nature of His everlasting intercession for us? (β) Does He continue to offer a true sacrifice in Heaven? (γ) How can His priesthood endure after the Last Judgment, when His intercession must of necessity cease?

α) Theologians are not agreed as to whether Christ's heavenly intercession for the human race is to be conceived as merely implicit (*interpretativa*), or as explicit (*formalis*).

The former view is held by Vasquez and Thomassin, the latter and more probable one by Petavius. As Christ actually prayed for us while on earth, there is no reason to assume that His continued intercession in Heaven is silent or merely implicit,— especially in view of the promise which He gave His Apostles that He would ask the Father to send them another Paraclete. Cfr. John XIV, 16: "And I will ask the Father, and he shall give you another Paraclete." Why weaken the term "ask" or "petition" (*rogare*, ἐρωτᾶν) to prop the

32 St. Ambrose, *In Luc.*, X, n. 170: *"Vulnera accepta pro nobis coelo inferre maluit, abolere noluit, ut Deo Patri nostrae pretia libertatis ostenderet."*

doubtful hypothesis that His intercession is merely virtual?

Certain of the Fathers seem to contradict the view defended by Petavius. But the construction put upon their utterances by Vasquez and Thomassin is untenable. In reality these Fathers merely wish to emphasize the fact that the theandric prayer of Jesus has none of the defects necessarily inherent in purely human prayer, such as indigence, a feeling of helplessness and guilt, an appeal to mercy, etc. The theandric intercession of our heavenly Advocate is based upon the infinite satisfaction which He has given for us, and hence is in no wise an humble supplication for grace, but a confident assertion of His merits on behalf of those whom He has redeemed. This is one of the reasons why the Church does not pray or instruct her children to pray: "Lord Jesus, intercede for us!" but: "Christ, hear us!" "Christ, have mercy on us!"[33]

β) Our second question, it may be well to premise, has nothing whatever to do with the Socinian error that Jesus offered no true sacrifice on earth but became the High Priest of humanity only after His Ascension into Heaven. Accepting the sacrificial character of His death, theologians merely ask: Does He continue to offer a true sacrifice for us in Heaven?

Thalhofer[34] answered this question in the affirmative, and his view has been adopted by L. Zill[35] and P.

33 Cfr. Franzelin, *De Verbo Incarnato*, thes. 51, n. iii; De Lugo, *De Myst. Incarnationis*, disp. 27, sect. 4, n. 61 sqq.

34 *Das Opfer des Alten und Neuen Bundes*, pp. 201 sqq., Ratisbon 1870.

35 *Der Brief an die Hebräer*, pp. 430 sqq., Mainz 1879.

Schoulza.[36] The purpose of these writers in taking the position they do is twofold: (1) to gain a basis for a reasonable explanation of the metaphysical essence of the Sacrifice of the Mass, and (2) to give a tangible content to the Scriptural teaching of Christ's eternal priesthood.

Thalhofer declares the formal element of sacrifice to consist, not in the exterior oblation of the victim, which is in some manner or other transformed, but solely in the interior disposition of the sacrificing priest. But this theory is contrary to the common teaching of Catholic divines and does not square with certain generally admitted facts. Granted that the disposition of the sacrificing priest is the intrinsic and invisible *forma,* and consequently the most important part of a sacrifice; yet it can never supply the extrinsic physical form. Christ's constant pointing to His wounds, of which Thalhofer makes so much, is merely a significant gesture which effects no intrinsic transformation of the kind strictly demanded by the notion of sacrifice. Zill attempted to construct a Scriptural basis for Thalhofer's theory, but his deductions had already been substantially refuted by Tournely in his argument against Faustus Socinus.[37] St. Paul, far from asserting that Christ offers sacrifice in Heaven, or that He continues His earthly sacrifice there, expressly declares that our Lord merely asserts *ad modum interpellationis* and forever the sacrifice He has once for all consummated on the Cross. This interpellation can in no wise be construed as a sacrifice.[38]

36 *Liturgia Catholica Fidei Magistra,* Insulis 1901.

37 Tournely, *De Incarn.,* qu. 5, art. 2; cfr. Franzelin, *De Verbo Incarnato,* p. 539.

38 Cfr. F. Stentrup, *Soteriologia,* thes. 82; Pesch, *Prael. Dogmat.,* Vol. IV, 3rd ed., pp. 300 sqq.

γ) There remains the third question: How can Christ's priesthood endure forever, since after the Last Judgment not only the hypothetical sacrifice construed by Thalhofer, but likewise His intercession for us must needs cease?

There can be no doubt whatever that our Lord's priestly intercession in Heaven will end with the last Mass celebrated on earth. Nevertheless, His priesthood will continue, in a threefold respect. (1) He will remain "a priest for ever" in dignity (*secundum dignitatem*), because His sacerdotal character stands or falls with the Hypostatic Union, and consequently is indelible and incapable of being lost.[39] (2) Christ's priesthood endures eternally in respect of its effectiveness (*secundum effectum*), in so far as the fruits of the sacrifice of the Cross are unceasingly renewed in the grace and glory enjoyed by the Elect in Heaven.[40] (3) Christ remains the eternal High Priest of humanity *secundum affectum;* for, while He does not offer up a perpetual sacrifice in the strict and proper sense of the term, He causes a sweet burnt-offering of unending adoration and thanksgiving to rise before the throne of the Most Holy Trinity,— which is after all the ultimate purpose and end of all creation.

39 Cfr. Thesis I, *supra,* pp. 127 sqq.

40 Cfr. St. Thomas, *S. Theol.,* 3a, qu. 22, art. 5: "*In officio sacerdotis duo possunt considerari: primo quidem ipsa oblatio sacrificii, secundo ipsa sacrificii consummatio, quae quidem consistit in hoc, quod illi pro quibus sacrificium offertur, finem sacrificii consequuntur. Finis autem sacrificii quod Christus obtulit, non fuerunt bona temporalia, sed aeterna, quae per eius mortem adipiscimur.*" *L. c.,* ad 2: "*Licet passio et mors Christi de caetero non sint iteranda, tamen virtus illius hostiae semel oblatae permanet in aeternum.*"

CHAPTER II

CHRIST'S PROPHETICAL OFFICE

1. Definition of the Term "Prophet."—The word "Prophet" is etymologically derived from the Greek verb πρόφημι, *to speak for some one,* then, *to foretell* (Hebr. רֹאֶה = *vates,* seer). In a wider sense it signifies a teacher (*magister,* διδάσκαλος; Hebr. נָבִיא = speaker, orator).[1]

The Bible employs the term Prophet in both meanings, most frequently however in the latter. Old Testament prophetism was not limited to extraordinary predictions of future events, but comprised primarily the ordinary teaching office, which was clothed with divine authority and exercised by instruction, admonition, warnings, and threats. The so-called prophetic schools of the Jews were colleges founded for the training of professional teachers of religion, not of prophets in the strict sense of the term.[2]

To say that Christ exercised the office or function of a prophet, is equivalent to saying that He possessed in the highest degree the gift of prophecy (*donum prophetiae*) and the vocation

1 Cfr. R. Cornely, *Comp. Intr. in N. T.*, 8th ed., p. 381.

2 Cfr. R. Cornely, *Introd. Spec. in Libros V. T.*, Vol. II, pp. 267 sqq., Paris 1887; Maas, *op. cit.*, Vol. I, 108 sqq.

of a teacher (*magisterium*). Soteriology deals with Him only as a teacher.

2. THE PROPHETIC TEACHING OFFICE OF CHRIST.—The Old Testament prophets hailed the future Messias as a teacher of truth, and when Jesus Christ appeared in Palestine, He actually exercised the functions of a teacher in the most exalted sense of the term.

a) Moses, who both as the founder of a religion and a teacher *par excellence*, is a prominent type of the Messias, uttered the famous prophecy registered in Deut. XVIII, 15: "The Lord thy God will raise up a prophet [3] of thy nation and of thy brethren like unto me: him thou shalt hear." [4] This passage is expressly applied to Christ in the New Testament.[5]

Isaias foretells that the coming Messias will deliver humanity from sin and error. Is. LXI, 1 sq.: "The spirit of the Lord is upon me, because the Lord hath anointed me: he hath sent me to preach to the meek, to heal the contrite of heart, and to preach a release to the captives, and deliverance to them that are shut up; to proclaim the acceptable year of the Lord, and the day of vengeance of our God: to comfort all that mourn."

Christ Himself publicly read this passage in the synagogue at Nazareth, and when he had folded the book,

3 נָבִיא.

4 Cfr. Deut. XVIII, 18.

5 Acts III, 22 sqq. "Be penitent, therefore, and be converted, that your sins may be blotted out; that when the times of refreshment shall come from the presence of the Lord, and he shall send him who hath been preached unto you, Jesus Christ, whom heaven indeed must receive, until the times of the restitution of all things, which God hath spoken by the mouth of his holy prophets, from the beginning of the world. For Moses said: A prophet shall the Lord your God raise up unto you of your brethren, like unto me: him you shall hear. . . ."

said (Luke IV, 21): "This day is fulfilled this scripture in your ears." [6]

b) The New Testament has confirmed the fulfilment of the Old Testament prophecies. It has also demonstrated their truth. When Jesus was engaged in recruiting His disciples, Philip said to Nathanael: "We have found him of whom Moses in the law, and the prophets did write, Jesus the son of Joseph of Nazareth." [7] It was with the utmost confidence that our Lord appealed to Moses: "Think not that I will accuse you to the Father. There is one that accuseth you, Moses, in whom you trust. For if you did believe Moses, you would perhaps believe me also; for he wrote of me." [8] After He had fed five thousand people with a few loaves of bread, those who had witnessed the miracle enthusiastically exclaimed: "This is of a truth the prophet that is to come into the world." [9] When He had raised the widow's son to life, there came a fear on those about Him, "and they glorified God, saying: A great prophet [10] is risen up among us; and, God hath visited his people." [11]

c) Christ exercised His teaching office by journeying about Palestine and preaching the glad tidings of salvation.

6 Cfr. Matth. V, 5.

7 John I, 45.

8 John V, 45 sq.

9 ὁ προφήτης ὁ ἐρχόμενος εἰς τὸν κόσμον. John VI, 14.

10 προφήτης μέγας.

11 Luke VII, 16.

St. Matthew records that "the people were in admiration at his doctrine; for he was teaching them as one having power, and not as the scribes and Pharisees."[12] He presented Himself as the absolute Teacher of truth. Cfr. John XVIII, 37: "For this was I born, and for this came I into the world, that I should give testimony to the truth." For it was "His Father" who spoke through Him,[13] and He Himself was "the way, and the truth, and the life."[14] Consequently, there can be no other teacher beside or above Him: "Neither be ye called masters; for one is your master,[15] Christ."[16] Acknowledging Him as the sovereign teacher of mankind, Nicodemus says: "Rabbi, we know that thou art come a teacher from God; for no man can do these signs which thou dost, unless God be with him."[17] Even so great a teacher as St. John the Baptist literally paled in the glorious halo which encircled the Divine Master: "He was not the light, but was to give testimony of the light."[18]

Nor must we forget the power of our Saviour's example, which more effectively even than His words prompted men to embrace the truth and lead a virtuous life. Fully realizing that "Example serves where precept fails," St. Luke in writing his Gospel, as he himself admits,[19] was chiefly concerned with the things which "Jesus began to do and to teach."[20] That it was the Redeemer's express purpose to set a good example is manifest from His own declaration in John XIII, 15: "For I have given you an example,[21] that as I have

12 Matth. VII, 28 sq.

13 Cfr. John XIV, 10; XVII, 8.

14 John XIV, 6.

15 *Magister*, καθηγήτης.

16 Matth. XXIII, 10. Cfr. John XIII, 13.

17 John III, 2.

18 John I, 8. Cfr. Pohle-Preuss, *Christology*, pp. 31 sqq.; H. Schell, *Jahve und Christus*, pp. 403 sqq., Paderborn 1905.

19 Acts I, 1.

20 ποιεῖν τε καὶ διδάσκειν.

21 ὑπόδειγμα.

done to you, so you do also." St. Paul strongly insists on the importance of our being made comformable to the image of the Son of God,[22] and did not rest until Christ had been formed in all his hearers.[23] Christ was the *beau-idéal* of virtue, because He was without sin; and His example was most effective, because He was impelled by supreme charity. This accounts for the inexhaustible power which flows from the imitation of Christ and never ceases to purify, ennoble, energize, and rejuvenate men and to lead them on to moral perfection. In confirmation of this truth we need but point to the lives of the Saints.[24]

d) For an adequate theological explanation of the singular greatness and perfection of Christ's prophetical office we must go to its fountain-head, the Hypostatic Union.

a) Endowed with a fulness of knowledge unparalleled in the history of the human race, Jesus was in a position to propound His teaching with absolute certainty and irresistible conviction.[25] Equipped with miraculous powers and the gift of prophecy, He was able to confirm and seal His words by signs and miracles. As the supernatural Head of grace, He was in the altogether unique position of one able to enlighten his hearers with the torch of faith and to fire their hearts with His grace. In all three of these respects He has absolutely no peer among men, and it is sheer folly to compare Him with Socrates

22 Rom. VIII, 29.

23 Gal. IV, 19.

24 Cfr. S. Raue, O. F. M., *Christus als Erzieher. Eine methodische Studie über das hl. Evangelium*, 2nd ed., Freiburg 1902. For the teaching of the Fathers consult Petavius, *De Incarn.*, II, 10; Stentrup, *Soteriologia*, thes. 134 sqq.

25 Cfr. Pohle-Preuss, *Christology*, pp. 249 sqq.

or even with the greatest of the prophets, Moses and John the Baptist.

β) Nor can it be urged as an argument against the sublimity of His prophetical office, that Jesus addressed Himself only to the Jews of Palestine. He had excellent reasons for confining His personal activity to that particular nation and country. We will enumerate four of the principal ones given by St. Thomas.[26] (1) He had to fulfil the promises which God had made to the Jews in the Old Testament. (2) It was becoming that the Gospel should reach the gentiles through the instrumentality of God's Chosen People. (3) Jesus had to pay due regard to the peculiar mentality of the Jewish nation. (4) The method He chose was better adapted than any other to demonstrate the triumphant power of the Cross. After His Resurrection He sent out His disciples to teach and baptize all nations, and when He had ascended into Heaven, He appointed a special Apostle for the gentiles. His teaching was as open and public as the scene of His activity. Unlike the pagan philosophers, He made no distinction between esoteric and exoteric truths. His motto was: "That which I tell you in the dark, speak ye in the light: and that which you hear in the ear, preach ye upon the housetops."[27]

γ) Our Divine Lord had very good reasons for disdaining to consign His heavenly teaching to books. It eminently befitted His high office as Teacher of mankind to employ the most perfect mode of teaching, namely oral instruction, which goes straight to the heart and reaches all, even those who are unable to read. It was for this same reason, in the opinion of St. Thomas, that He commanded His Church to instruct by word of mouth

26 *S. Theol.*, 3a, qu. 42, art. 1.

27 Matth. X, 27. Cfr. St. Thomas, *S. Theol.*, 3a, qu. 42, art. 3.

and constituted oral tradition a source of faith side by side with Sacred Scripture. Some of the wisest men of antiquity (*e. g.*, Socrates and Pythagoras) exercised a tremendous influence over succeeding generations without ever having recourse to the stylus or the pen. Oral instruction was admirably adapted to the propagation of Christianity. Had our Lord presented His teaching in the form of bookish lore, consigned to parchment or papyrus, it would have become a veritable apple of discord. Then again, in the words of St. Thomas, "those who refused to believe what the Apostles wrote, would not have believed Christ Himself had He consigned His doctrines to writing." [28]

3. THE ECCLESIASTICAL MAGISTERIUM A CONTINUATION OF CHRIST'S PROPHETICAL OFFICE. —As the priesthood of our Divine Lord is continued on earth by the celebration of the Holy Sacrifice of the Mass and the administration of the Sacraments, especially Holy Orders, so His prophetic office is continued by the magisterium of the Catholic Church.

a) The very fact that Christ established a Church to teach "all nations" shows that He wished her to continue His prophetical office. He guaranteed her His special assistance and promised to be with her "all days, even to the consummation of the world." [29] Having established her as a teacher, He sent her the Spirit of Truth, who

28 *S. Theol., l. c.*—On the apocryphal correspondence between our Lord and Abgar, King of Edessa, cfr. R. A. Lipsius, *Die edessenische Abgarsage kritisch untersucht*, Braunschweig 1880; J. Tixeront *Les Origines de l'Église d'Edesse et la Légende d'Abgar*, Paris 1888; H. Leclerq, art. "Abgar" in the *Catholic Encyclopedia*, Vol. I, pp. 42 sq.

29 Matth. XXVIII, 20.

informs and vivifies her as the soul informs and actuates the body, and enables her to keep the deposit of faith intact against all attempts at diminution or distortion. Thus the infallibility of the Church and of her Supreme Pontiff ultimately rests upon the prophetic office of Christ Himself, who is the infallible source and teacher of all truth.[30]

b) This explains why the Church participates in the prerogatives of the prophetic office as exercised by her Divine Founder. As the faithful custodian of the deposit of faith she teaches the whole truth. There is no higher magisterium conceivable than hers. The "spiritual church" expected by the Montanists and the "Johannine church" imagined by some modern heretics are pure figments. Christianity is the absolute religion and cannot be measured by the inadequate yardstick of comparative science. The Catholic Church, through her connexion with Jesus Christ and the Holy Ghost, enjoys a truly divine authority, by which she proclaims with infallible certainty the dogmas of faith and morals and condemns heretical errors whenever the necessity arises. Her anathemas are as truly binding on all men as her dogmatic definitions. Finally, she is endowed with unlimited adaptability, which enables her to adjust herself to all times and circumstances, provided they do not run counter to the orthodox faith and the eternal principles of true morality. No matter how times may change, the Catholic Church, ever old and ever young, fills them with her own spirit, overcomes error and sin, and directs all legitimate efforts for the betterment of the race into their divinely appointed channels. There is no error so novel,

30 Cfr. P. J. Toner, art. "Infallibility" in the *Catholic Encyclopedia*, Vol. VII, pp. 790 sqq.; J. Pohle, art. "Unfehlbarkeit" in Herder's *Kirchenlexikon*, Vol. XII, pp. 24? sqq.

no intellectual malady so grave that the Church is not able to counteract it with antidotes from her spiritual pharmacopœia. Our own time furnishes a most instructive exemplification of this truth. It is a period of transition and fermentation. Pius X has vigorously condemned the Modernistic errors endangering the faith, and there is no doubt that they can be effectively warded off if the nations will listen to the voice of Holy Mother Church.[31]

31 Cfr. H. Pesch, S. J., *Die soziale Befähigung der Kirche*, 3d ed., Berlin 1911.

CHAPTER III

CHRIST'S KINGSHIP

1. DEFINITION OF THE TERM.—The word king (*rex*, βασιλεύς,) denotes a sovereign invested with supreme authority over a nation, country or tribe.

a) Kingship includes three separate and distinct functions: legislative, judiciary, and executive, which together constitute the supreme power of jurisdiction or government.

The royal *dominium iurisdictionis* must not be confounded with what is known as the right of ownership (*dominium proprietatis*). The latter is directed to the possession of impersonal objects, while the former implies the governance of free persons or subjects. The two differ both logically and in fact, and neither can be directly deduced from the other. The ruling power of a king or emperor by no means implies the possession of property rights either in his subjects or their belongings. The subjects of a monarch are as free to possess private property as the monarch himself, not to speak of the right of personal liberty.

It may be well to observe, however, that these limitations apply to earthly kings only. God, being the Creator and Lord of the universe, is the absolute owner of all things, including men and their belongings.[1]

b) The royal power with its various functions may be either secular or spiritual. The former is instituted for man's earthly, the latter for his spiritual benefit. Christ's is a spiritual kingdom, and will continue as such throughout eternity. Holy Scripture and the Church frequently liken His kingship to the office of a shepherd, to emphasize the loving care with which He rules us and provides for our necessities.

2. CHRIST'S EARTHLY KINGSHIP AS TAUGHT IN SACRED SCRIPTURE.—Both the Old and the New Testament represent our Lord Jesus Christ as a true King, who descended upon this terrestrial planet to establish a spiritual kingdom. This kingdom is the Catholic Church. Christ did not come as a worldly monarch, but as "the bishop of our souls." [2]

a) If we examine the Messianic prophecies of the Old Testament we find the kingdom of Israel, or "throne of David," represented as a type of the Messianic kingdom that was to come. Cfr. 2 Kings VII, 12 sq.: "I will raise up thy [David's] seed after thee, which shall proceed out of thy bowels, and I will establish his kingdom. He shall build a house [*i. e.,* temple, church] to my name, and I will establish the throne of

1 Cfr. Pohle-Preuss. *God: His Knowability, Essence and Attributes,* pp. 286 sqq.

2 Cfr. 1 Pet. II, 25.

his kingdom for ever." The same prediction is made in Psalms II, XXX, XXXVII, XLV, LXXII, and CIX. Isaias,[3] Daniel,[4] and Zacharias[5] depict the Messias in glowing colours as a Ruler, as the Prince of peace and the mighty General of a great army. These prophecies were all fulfilled, though not in the manner anticipated by the carnal-minded Jews. The Messias came as a King, but not with the pomp of an earthly sovereign, nor for the purpose of freeing the Jewish nation from the yoke of its oppressors.

Nevertheless the New Testament hails the lowly infant born of the Blessed Virgin as a great King. Even before his birth the Archangel informs His Mother that "The Lord God shall give unto him the throne of David his father, and he shall reign in the house of Jacob for ever."[6] The wise men hurried to His manger from the far East and anxiously inquired: "Where is he that is born king of the Jews?"[7] Yet when, after the miraculous multiplication of loaves, the Jews tried to "take him by force and make him king," Jesus "fled again into the mountain himself alone."[8] And when, in the face of death, Pilate asked Him: "Art thou a king then?" He answered: "Thou sayest that I am a king."[9] After they had crucified Him, "they put over his head his cause written: This is Jesus the King of the Jews."[10] Sorely disappointed in their worldly hopes, and still enmeshed in political ambitions, the two disciples who went to Emmaus lamented: "But we hoped, that it was he that should have redeemed Israel."[11]

3 Is. IX, 6 sqq., 11.
4 Dan. VII, 13 sqq.
5 Zach. IX.
6 Luke I, 32 sq.
7 Matth. II, 2.
8 John VI, 15.
9 John XVIII, 37.
10 Matth. XXVII, 37.
11 Luke XXIV, 21. Cfr. Acts I, 6.

b) This seeming contradiction between the Old Testament prophecies and the actual life of our Lord Jesus Christ finds its solution in the Church's teaching that His is a purely spiritual kingdom. Cfr. Is. LX, 18 sqq.; Jer. XXIII, 5 sqq.; Ezech. XXXVII, 21 sqq. For the sake of greater clearness, it will be advisable to separate the *quaestio iuris* from the *quaestio facti,* and to treat each on its own merits.

α) The *quaestio facti.*— Taking the facts as we know them, there can be no doubt that Christ never intended to establish an earthly kingdom. He fled when the Jews attempted to make him king.[12] He acknowledged the Roman Emperor as the legitimate ruler of Palestine and commanded the Jews to "render to Cæsar the things that are Cæsar's, and to God the things that are God's." [13] He consistently refused to interfere in secular affairs, as when he said to the man who asked Him to adjudicate a question of inheritance: "Who hath appointed me judge, or divider, over you?" [14] And He expressly declared before Pilate:[15] "My kingdom is not of this world. If my kingdom were of this world, my servants would certainly strive that I should not be delivered to the Jews: but now my kingdom is not from hence." [16]

β) The *quaestio iuris.*— What first strikes us from the juridic point of view is: Did Christ merely refrain from asserting His legal claim to secular kingship, or

12 John VI, 15.

13 Matth. XXII, 21.

14 Luke XII, 14.

15 John XVIII, 36.

16 Cfr. Ferd. Stentrup, *Soteriologia,* thes. 138. For a critical refutation of Loisy's errors see M. Lepin, *Christ and the Gospel* (English tr.), Philadelphia 1910, especially pp. 475 sqq.

had He no such claim, at least *in actu primo?* Catholic theologians agree that as "the Son of David" Christ possessed no dynastic title to the kingdom of Juda; first, because His Messianic kingdom extended far beyond the limits of Palestine, in fact embraced the whole world; and secondly, because neither the Blessed Virgin Mary nor St. Joseph, though both descended from the "house of David," had any hereditary claim to the throne which had been irretrievably lost under Jechonias.[17] There is another point on which theologians are also of one mind. By virtue of His spiritual kingship the Godman possesses at least indirect power over all secular affairs, for else His spiritual power could not be conceived as absolutely unlimited, which would have imperiled the purpose of the Incarnation. This indirect power over worldly affairs is technically known as *potestas indirecta in temporalia.*

Its counterpart is the *potestas directa in temporalia,* and in regard to this there exists a long-drawn-out controversy among theologians. Gregory of Valentia and Cardinal Bellarmine[18] hold that Christ had no direct jurisdiction in secular or temporal matters, while Suarez[19] and De Lugo[20] maintain that He had. The affirmative opinion appeals to us as more probable, though the Scriptural texts marshalled in its favor by De Lugo[21] cannot be said to be absolutely convincing. These texts (Matth. XXVIII, 18; Acts X, 36; 1 Cor. XV, 27; Apoc. I, 5 and XIX, 16) can be explained partly by the doctrine of the *communicatio idiomatum,*[22] partly by reference to our Lord's spiritual kingdom. De Lugo's *theological* arguments, however, are very strong

17 Cfr. Jer. XXII, 30.

18 *De Rom. Pontifice,* V, 4 sq.

19 *De Myst. Vitae Christi,* disp. 42, sect. 2.

20 *De Myst. Incarn.,* disp. 30, § 1.

21 *L. c.,* n. 5.

22 Cfr. Pohle-Preuss, *Christology,* pp. 184 sqq.

indeed. Take this one, for example. Christ's direct jurisdiction in matters temporal is based on the Hypostatic Union. On account of the Hypostatic Union His sacred humanity was entitled to such excellencies and prerogatives as the power of working miracles, the fulness of knowledge, the highest measure of the beatific vision, the dignity of headship over all creatures,[23] etc. And it is but reasonable to conclude that there must have been due to Him in a similar way that other prerogative which we may call kingship over all creatures.[24] From this point of view it may be argued that the theandric dignity of our Lord, flowing from the Hypostatic Union, gave Him an imprescriptible claim to royal power, so that, had He willed, He could have deposed all the kings and princes of this world and constituted Himself the Head of a universal monarchy.

Bellarmine's apprehension that this teaching might exert a pernicious influence on the papacy, is absolutely groundless. For, in the first place, Christ's vice-gerent on earth is not Christ Himself, and secondly, the prerogatives and powers enjoyed by our Lord, even those of a purely spiritual nature, are not *eo ipso* enjoyed by the Pope. "Christ was able to do many things in the spiritual realm," rightly observes De Lugo, "which the Pope cannot do; for example, institute sacraments, confer grace through other than sacramental channels, etc."[25]

These considerations also explain why Christ declared Himself legally exempt from the obligation of paying taxes and "paid the didrachmas" solely to avoid scandal.[26]

23 Cfr. Pohle-Preuss, *Christology*, pp. 239 sqq.

24 De Lugo, *l. c.*, n. 8.

25 *L. c.*, n. 11.

26 Cfr. Matth. XVII, 23 sqq.

The question as to the property rights enjoyed by our Divine Saviour may be solved by the same principle which we have applied to that of His temporal jurisdiction. Vasquez was inconsistent in rejecting De Lugo's solution of the former problem after accepting his view of the latter.[27] For, while it is perfectly true that the Godman never laid claim to earthly goods, but lived in such abject poverty that He literally "had not where to lay his head,"[28] this does not argue that He had no legal right to acquire worldly possessions. The simple truth is that He had renounced this right for good reasons.

It is an article of faith, defined by Pope John XXII in his Constitution "*Quum inter nonnullos,*" that Christ actually possessed at least a few things as His personal property.[29]

3. Christ's Heavenly Kingship, or the Dogma of His Ascension and Sitting at the Right Hand of the Father.—The Resurrection of our Lord and His Descent into hell merely formed the preliminaries of His kingly office. It was by His glorious Ascension that He took formal possession of His royal throne in Heaven, which Holy Scripture describes as "sitting at the right hand of God." Both His Ascension and His sitting at the right hand of God are fundamental articles of faith, as may be judged from the fact that they have been incorporated into the Apostles' Creed.

27 *De Incarn.*, disp. 87, cap. 6.

28 Luke IX. 58. Cfr. St. Thomas, *Summa Theol.*, 3a, qu. 40, art. 3.

29 Denzinger-Bannwart, n. 494.

a) There is no need of entering into a detailed Scriptural argument to prove these dogmas. Our Lord Himself clearly predicted His Ascension into Heaven,[30] and the prophecy was fulfilled in the presence of many witnesses. Mark XVI, 19: "And the Lord Jesus, after He had spoken to them, was taken up into heaven, and sitteth on the right hand of God." [31]

The argument from Tradition is copiously developed by Suarez in the 51st disputation of his famous treatise *De Mysteriis Vitae Christi.*

Our Lord "ascended by His own might," says the Roman Catechism, "and was not raised aloft by the power of another, as was Elias, who 'went up' in a fiery chariot into heaven (4 Kings II, 11), or as was the prophet Habacuc (Dan. XIV, 35 sqq.), or Philip the deacon (Acts VIII, 39), who, borne through the air by the divine power, traversed far distant parts of the earth. Neither did He ascend into heaven solely as God, by the supreme power of the Divinity, but also as man; for although the Ascension could not have taken place by natural power, yet that virtue with which the blessed soul of Christ had been endowed, was capable of moving the body as it pleased; and his body, now glorified, readily obeyed the command of the actuating soul. And thus we believe that Christ, as God and man, ascended by His own power into heaven." [32]

The phrase, "sitteth on the right hand of God," must not, of course, be interpreted literally, since with God there is neither right nor left. It is a figurative expression, intended to denote the exalted station occupied

30 John VI, 63; XIV, 1 sqq.; XVI, 28.

31 Ὁ μὲν οὖν κύριος Ἰησοῦς μετὰ τὸ λαλῆσαι αὐτοῖς ἀνηλήμφθη εἰς τὸν οὐρανὸν καὶ ἐκάθισεν ἐκ δεξιῶν τοῦ Θεοῦ.

32 *Cat. Rom.*, P. I, c. 7, qu. 2. Cfr. S. Thomas, *S. Theol.*, 3a, qu. 57, art. 1.

by our Lord in heaven,[33] and also His calm, immutable possession of glory and jurisdiction over the whole universe.[34] It is in His capacity of royal judge that Jesus will one day reappear with great power and majesty "to judge the living and the dead." [35]

b) The two dogmas under consideration have both a Christological and a Soteriological bearing.

α) From the Christological point of view our Saviour's Ascension as well as His sitting on the right hand of the Father signalize the beginning, or rather the continuation, of the *status exaltationis,* of which His Resurrection and Descent into hell were mere preludes. His humiliation (*status exinanitionis*) in the "form of a servant," [36] His poverty, suffering, and death, made way for an eternal kingship in Heaven. The truly regal splendor of our Divine Redeemer during and after His Ascension is more strongly emphasized in the Apostolic Epistles than in the Gospels. In the Epistles the epithet "Lord" (*Dominus,* ὁ κύριος) nearly always connotes royal dominion. Cfr. 1 Tim. VI, 15: "Who is the Blessed and only Mighty, King of kings, and Lord of lords." It is only since His Ascension into Heaven that Christ rules the universe conjointly with the Father, though this joint dominion will not reach its highest perfection till the day of the Last Judgment, when all creation will lie in absolute subjection "under His feet." [37]

β) From the Soteriological point of view it would be wrong to represent Christ's Ascension (not to speak of His Resurrection and Descent into hell) as the total or

33 Cfr. Heb. I, 13.

34 Cfr. Eph. I, 20 sqq.

35 Cfr. St. Thomas, *S. Theol.,* 3a, qu. 58.

36 Cfr. Pohle-Preuss, *Christology,* pp. 95 sq.

37 Cfr. Eph. I, 22 sqq.; Heb. II, 8.

even partial cause (*causa meritoria*) of our Redemption. The atonement was effected solely by the sacrifice of the Cross. Nevertheless St. Paul writes: "Jesus . . . entered . . . into heaven itself, that he may appear now in the presence of God for us." [38] In other words, He continues to exercise His mediatorial office in Heaven. How are we to understand this? St. Thomas explains it as follows: "Christ's Ascension is the cause of our salvation in a twofold way, first on our part, and secondly on His. On our part, in so far as His Ascension directs our minds to Him. . . . On His part, in so far as He ascended for our salvation, (1) to prepare for us the way to Heaven, . . . (2) because Christ entered Heaven, as the High Priest entered the Holy of holies, to make intercession for us; [39] . . . (3) in order that, seated as Lord God on the throne of Heaven, He might thence send us divine gifts." [40] As is apparent from the last-mentioned two points, Christ's kingship is closely bound up with His priesthood. In fact it may be said in a general way that the three functions or offices of our Divine Redeemer are so closely intertwined that they cannot be separated.

For the special benefit of canonists we would observe that the threefold character of these functions furnishes no adequate basis for the current division of the power of the Church into *potestas ordinis, potestas magisterii,* and *potestas iurisdictionis*.[41] The traditional division into *potestas ordinis* and *potestas iurisdictionis* is the only adequate and correct one from the dogmatic point of view.[42]

38 *νῦν ἐμφανισθῆναι τῷ προσώπῳ τοῦ Θεοῦ ὑπὲρ ἡμῶν*. Heb. IX, 24.

39 Heb. VII, 25.

40 *S. Theol.*, 3a, qu. 57, art. 6.

41 This division is employed by Walter, Phillips, Richter, Hinschius, and others.

42 Cfr. Scheeben, *Dogmatik*, Vol.

4. Christ's Kingship as Continued in His Church on Earth.—We have shown that our Divine Redeemer did not claim secular or temporal jurisdiction. It follows *a fortiori* that the Church which He has established is a purely spiritual kingdom and must confine herself to the government of souls.

a) The Catholic Church was not established as a political power. She represents that peaceful Messianic kingdom which was foreshadowed by the Old Testament prophets and which the Prince of Peace founded with His Precious Blood. Hence the hierarchical order displayed in the papacy, episcopate, priesthood, and diaconate, is purely spiritual. Hence, too, the means of sanctification which the Church employs (prayer, sacrifice, and the sacraments) are of an exclusively spiritual character. Christ, who was the King of Kings, did not disturb the earthly monarchs of His time in their jurisdiction, and it cannot be the mission of His Church to grasp at political power or treat temporal rulers as her vassals. Hers is a purely spiritual dominion for the sanctification of souls.

Being God's kingdom on earth, the Church exists in and for this world, but is not of it. The theory of a few medieval canonists that she enjoys direct jurisdiction over all nations and rulers, has no foundation either in Sacred Scripture or in history. It is unevangelical for the reason that Christ never claimed such power. It is unhistorical because the "donation of Constantine," on which it rests, is a fiction.[43] This theory, which was

I, p. 67, Freiburg 1873; Cavagnis, *Instit. Iuris Publ. Ecclesiae,* 4th ed., Vol. I, p. 24, Rome 1906.

43 Cfr. L. Duchesne, *The Beginnings of the Temporal Sovereignty of the Popes* (English tr.), p. 120,

inspired by the imposing phenomenon of the Holy Roman Empire, has never been adopted by the Church, nor is it maintained by the majority of her theologians and canonists. The relation between Church and State still remains a knotty problem.[44] Harnack seriously distorts the truth when he says: "The Roman Church in this way privily pushed itself into the place of the Roman world-empire, of which it is the actual continuation; the empire has not perished, but has only undergone a transformation. If we assert, and mean the assertion to hold good even of the present time, that the Roman Church is the old Roman Empire consecrated by the Gospel, that is no mere 'clever remark,' but the recognition of the true state of the matter historically, and the most appropriate and fruitful way of describing the character of this Church. It still governs the nations; its popes rule like Trajan and Marcus Aurelius; Peter and Paul have taken the place of Romulus and Remus; the bishops and archbishops, of the proconsuls; the troops of priests and monks correspond to the legions; the Jesuits, to the imperial body-guard. The continued influence of the old Empire and its institutions may be traced in detail, down to individual legal ordinances, nay, even in the very clothes. That is no church like the evangelical communities, or the national churches of the East; it is a political creation, and as imposing as a world-empire, because the continuation of the Roman Empire." [45] The possession of political power may be useful, nay, relatively speaking, necessary to insure to the Pope the free and untrammelled exercise of his spiritual functions; but

London 1908; J. P. Kirsch in the *Catholic Encyclopedia*, Vol. V, pp. 118 sqq.

44 Cfr. J. Pohle in Herder's *Kirchenlexikon*, Vol. XII, 229 sqq.

45 *Das Wesen des Christentums*, p. 157, Leipzig 1902 (English tr.: *What is Christianity?* p. 270, 2nd ed., New York 1908).

it does not enter into the essence of the papacy, which for centuries has flourished without it and still commands the highest respect in spite of its spoliation by the Italian government.

b) The Church exercises a truly royal dominion over the souls of men, and hence must be entitled to all the prerogatives of a spiritual kingship. That is to say, within the limits of her divinely ordained constitution, she possesses legislative as well as judicial power over her members, including the executive right of inflicting punishment.[46] There can be no exercise of judicial power without the power of compulsion (*potestas coactiva s. vindicativa*) and it is, moreover, a formally defined dogma that the Church possesses this power.[47]

The penalties which she is authorized to inflict are, of course, predominantly spiritual (penitential acts, ecclesiastical censures, and especially excommunication).[48] But she can also impose temporal and bodily punishments (*poenae temporales et corporales*). We know that she has exercised this power, and it would be temerarious to deny that she possesses it.[49]

Has the Church also the power to put malefactors to death (*ius gladii*)? Canonists are not agreed on this point, though all admit that if the Church decides to inflict the death penalty, the sentence must be carried

46 Cfr. Matth. XVI, 19; XVIII, 15 sqq.

47 Cfr. Denzinger-Bannwart, *Enchiridion*, n. 499, 640, 1504 sq.

48 Cfr. 1 Cor. IV, 21; V, 5; 2 Cor. XIII, 1 sq.; 1 Tim. I, 20.

49 Cfr. Bouix, *De Iudic.*, Vol. I, p. 66, Paris 1855.

out by the secular power (*brachium saeculare*), because it would be unbecoming for the Spouse of Christ to stain her hands with blood, even if a deadly crime had been perpetrated against her.

It is a historical fact that the Church has never pronounced (much less, of course, executed) the death sentence or claimed the right to inflict it. Whenever, in the Middle Ages, she found herself constrained to pronounce judgment for a crime which the secular power was wont to punish by death (*e. g.* voluntary and obstinate heresy), she invariably turned the culprit over to the State. The cruel practice of burning heretics has fortunately ceased and will never be revived.

Regarded from the standpoint of religious principle, the question of the *ius gladii* is purely academic. The great majority of canonists seem to hold that the Church does not possess the right of inflicting capital punishment. The contrary teaching of Tarquini and De Luca [50] has occasioned much unfavorable criticism, and Cavagnis undoubtedly voices the conviction of most contemporary canonists when he says [51] that the so-called *ius gladii* has no solid basis either in Scripture or Tradition. Our Divine Redeemer did not approve the infliction of capital punishment,[52] nay, He restrained His followers from inflicting bodily injury.[53] St. Paul, in spite of his severity, never took recourse to any but spiritual measures. The great Pope Nicholas I said: "God's holy Church has no other sword than the spiritual; she does not kill, she dispenses life." [54] Her kingdom is purely spiritual,

50 *Inst. Iuris Eccl. Publ.*, Vol. I, pp. 261 sqq., Rome 1901.

51 *Inst. Iuris Publ. Eccl.*, 4th ed., Vol. I, pp. 190 sqq., Rome 1906.

52 Cfr. Luke IX, 53 sqq.

53 Cfr. Matth. XXVI, 52.

54 *"Sancta Dei Ecclesia gladium non habet nisi spiritualem, non occidit, sed vivificat."* (*Decr. Grat.*, c. 6, causa 33, qu. 2.)

and hence she must leave the infliction of capital punishment to the secular power.[55]

The most determined opponent of the Church's royal office is modern Liberalism, which employs all the powers of civil government to obstruct the exercise of her spiritual jurisdiction or to circumscribe that jurisdiction as narrowly as possible. Among the means invented for this purpose are the so-called *ius circa sacra,* the *appellatio tamquam ab abusu,*[56] and the *placetum regium,*[57]—in a word the whole iniquitous system known in English-speaking countries as Cæsaropapism or Erastianism[58] and based on the pernicious fallacy that the State is supreme in ecclesiastical affairs.

Readings:—* St. Thomas, *Summa Theologica,* 3a, qu. 22, and the Commentators.— A. Charre, *Le Sacrifice de l'Homme-Dieu,* Paris 1899.—* V. Thalhofer, *Das Opfer des Alten und Neuen Bundes,* Ratisbon 1870.— Idem, *Die Opferlehre des Hebräerbriefes,* Dillingen 1855.— W. Schenz, *Die priesterliche Tätigkeit des Messias nach dem Propheten Isaias,* Ratisbon 1892.— J. Grimal, *Le Sacerdoce et le Sacrifice de Notre Seigneur Jésus-Christ,* Paris 1908 (English tr. by M. J. Keyes, *The Priesthood and Sacrifice of Our Lord Jesus Christ,* Philadelphia 1915).—* Fr. Schmid, *Christus als Prophet, nach den Evangelien darge-*

55 Cfr. A. Vermeersch, S. J., *Tolerance* (tr. by W. H. Page), pp. 58 sqq., London 1913; J. Pohle, art. "Toleration" in the *Catholic Encyclopedia,* Vol. XIV; J. Keating, S. J., in *The Month,* No. 582, pp. 607 sqq.

56 Cfr. R. L. Burtsell in the *Catholic Encyclopedia,* Vol. I, pp. 650 sqq.

57 Cfr. S. Luzio in the *Catholic Encyclopedia, s. v.* "Exequatur," Vol. V, pp. 707 sq.

58 On the true meaning of this loosely used term see B. Ward in the *Catholic Encyclopedia,* Vol. V, pp. 514 sqq.

stellt, Brixen 1892.— Tanner, S. J., *Cruentum Christi Sacrificium, Incruentum Missae Sacrificium Explicatum,* Prague 1669.— B. Bartmann, *Das Himmelreich und sein König nach den Synoptikern,* Paderborn 1904.— A. J. Maas, S. J., *Christ in Type and Prophecy,* 2 vols., New York 1893–5.— M. Lepin, *Christ and the Gospel, or Jesus the Messiah and Son of God,* Philadelphia 1910. — Wilhelm-Scannell, *A Manual of Catholic Theology,* Vol. II, pp. 196–207, 2nd ed., London 1901.— W. Humphrey, S. J., *The One Mediator,* pp. 1–41, London *s. a.*— P. Batiffol, *L'Enseignement de Jésus,* Paris 1906.— J. H. Newman, *Sermons Bearing on Subjects of the Day,* New Impression, London 1898, pp. 52–62.—Other authorities quoted in the foot-notes.—M. D'Arcey, S. J., *Christ, Priest and Redeemer,* London and New York, 1928.

APPENDIX

THE ATONEMENT IN ITS RELATION TO GOD'S IMMUTABILITY

(See page 39)

There is another objection to the doctrine of Christ's vicarious atonement which deserves a brief refutation because it has seemed so strong to at least one Catholic writer (Schell) that it has led him to substitute a new and false conception of the atonement for the traditional one of Catholic theology. This objection is based on the immutability of the Divine Essence and may be formulated as follows: The atonement implies a change of mind or heart in God, but there can be no change in God because He is *actus purissimus*.

To assume a real change of mind or heart in God as a result of the atonement would indeed contradict the dogma of His immutability. But there is no such change involved in the dogma of the atonement, rightly understood. As the sun by means of the same rays produces contrary effects, *e. g.* melts ice and dries out a swamp, according to the differing quality of matter, so the immutable will of God either hates or loves man according as his moral state renders him worthy or unworthy of divine favor. The change involved in the process of justification, therefore, is not in the least a change on the part of God, but entirely on the part of the sinner. God immutably loves that which is good and holy, whereas the sinner changes from evil to good. When we say that the passion of Our Lord "appeased" the divine wrath, we do not mean that it affected God after the manner of a real cause or motive and induced Him to change His mind or will. The divine intellect and the divine will are predetermined in and by themselves from all eternity and admit no external influence. In speaking of a reconciliation of God or the appeasement of His wrath, the Church and her theologians merely adapt themselves to the understanding of the people, and what they mean to inculcate is that the redemption of the human race was predetermined by God from all eternity solely on condition that adequate satisfaction would be given by the Godman. No matter whether the future Redemption be conceived as an absolute or as a hypothetical result of God's predetermination, there is no trenching upon His immutability, because He inevitably foresaw the fulfilment or non-fulfilment of the condition and arranged His eternal plan of salvation accordingly. In the objective order of things God can will a future event either immutably in itself, or in connection with and as a consequence of some other event, which is related to the first as a cause to its effect. The causes involved in such a hypothetical decree of the divine will operate entirely outside of the Divine Essence without in any wise influencing or changing that Essence.[1]

1 See the chapter on "God's Immutability" in the first volume of this series, *God: His Knowability, Essence, and Attributes*, pp. 298-305, and P. Stufler's paper, "*Die Erlösungstat Christi in ihrer Beziehung zu Gott*," in the Innsbruck *Zeitschrift für katholische Theologie*, 1906, pp. 385 sqq.

INDEX

D

E

F

G

H

I